Cambridge Elements ≡

Elements in the Renaissance
edited by
John Henderson
Birkbeck, University of London, and Wolfson College, University of Cambridge
Jonathan K. Nelson
Syracuse University Florence, and Kennedy School, Harvard University

PARADOXES OF INEQUALITY IN RENAISSANCE ITALY

Samuel K. Cohn, Jr
University of Glasgow

CAMBRIDGE
UNIVERSITY PRESS

CAMBRIDGE
UNIVERSITY PRESS

University Printing House, Cambridge CB2 8BS, United Kingdom

One Liberty Plaza, 20th Floor, New York, NY 10006, USA

477 Williamstown Road, Port Melbourne, VIC 3207, Australia

314–321, 3rd Floor, Plot 3, Splendor Forum, Jasola District Centre,
New Delhi – 110025, India

103 Penang Road, #05–06/07, Visioncrest Commercial, Singapore 238467

Cambridge University Press is part of the University of Cambridge.

It furthers the University's mission by disseminating knowledge in the pursuit of
education, learning, and research at the highest international levels of excellence.

www.cambridge.org
Information on this title: www.cambridge.org/9781108970389
DOI: 10.1017/9781108980586

© Samuel K. Cohn, Jr 2021

First published 2021

A catalogue record for this publication is available from the British Library.

ISBN 978-1-108-97038-9 Paperback
ISSN 2631-9101 (online)
ISSN 2631-9098 (print)

Paradoxes of Inequality in Renaissance Italy

Elements in the Renaissance

DOI: 10.1017/9781108980586
First published online: July 2021

Samuel K. Cohn, Jr
University of Glasgow

Author for correspondence: Samuel K. Cohn, Jr, Samuel.Cohn@Glasgow.ac.uk

Abstract: This Element explores the longest spell that can be computed from quantifiable fiscal records when the gap between rich and poor narrowed: the post–Black Death century (c.1375 to c.1475). Paradoxically, with economic equality and prosperity on the rise, peasants, artisans, and shopkeepers suffered losses in political representation and status within cultural spheres. Threatened by growing economic equality after the Black Death, elites preserved and then enhanced their political, social, and cultural distinction predominantly through non-economic means and within political and cultural spheres. By investigating the interactions between three 'elements' – economics, politics, and culture – this Element presents new facets in the emergence of early Renaissance society in Italy.

Keywords: Black Death, late Middle Ages, Renaissance, inequality, non-elites

ISBNs: 9781108970389 (PB), 9781108980586 (OC)
ISSNs: 2631-9101 (online), 2631-9098 (print)

Contents

1 Economic Equality and Prosperity in the Post–Black Death Century

Preface

Demographic and economic historians have recently discovered an overriding trend: except for brief moments, inequality across Europe increased inexorably from the late Middle Ages to the present. However, the longest spell when the gap between rich and poor turned in the opposite direction and that can be demonstrated quantitatively with fiscal sources was the post–Black Death century (*c.*1375 to 1475).[1] The political and cultural consequences of this remarkable century remain to be unravelled. In short, this Element maintains that elites in late medieval and Renaissance Italy reacted to these new pressures from below not exclusively or primarily within the economic sphere.

In some parts of Europe – most prominently Eastern Europe and England – historians have long argued that elites did react economically to the new realities of labour scarcity by immediately imposing harsher forms of labour exploitation and restrictions on labour mobility to counter labour's new-born advantages. However, as will be reviewed in Section 2, historians now challenge most of these exceptional twists from the general European pattern. In addition, for several decades historians have shown that England's Ordinances and Statutes of Labourers of 1349 and 1351 failed to halt the rise in nominal wages. As John Munro has shown, post–Black Death real wages[2] into the fifteenth century rose by the same percentages in England as in the Low Countries, where no national wage restrictions and few municipal ones were promulgated (Cohn, 2007; Munro, 1994).

By contrast, elite reactions in Italy to the new economic realities created by Black Death demographics have not figured prominently in larger European discussions such as the Brenner debate or within Italian historiography. This Element argues that elites in central and northern Italy during the post–Black Death century colluded with the church and states to find other avenues to blunt the status of peasants, artisans, and shopkeepers, thereby preserving, and even enhancing, the social distinctions that widened the cultural gulf between them and commoners. Historians have yet, however, to investigate the price non-elites paid for their economic success following the Black Death. At the moment of their gains in the economic sphere, artisans' powers and prestige in a second sphere – politics – dwindled, as marked by the declining power of

---

[1] Some begin that century with the Black Death itself. See numerous articles and working papers by Guido Alfani and his équipe at Bocconi University, Milan: Alfani, 2021; Alfani and Di Tullio, 2019; and further studies: Pamuk, 2007; and Van Zanden, 1995.

[2] Wages controlled for inflation.

their guilds and their participation in larger legislative assemblies. Moreover, a third sphere of losses points to the cultural domain, at least as can be currently seen from research in late medieval and early Renaissance Tuscany and Umbria. By the end of the fourteenth century, non-elites' prerogatives to commission works of art that previously had preserved their lasting remembrance before God and their neighbours within ecclesiastic buildings had dwindled and began to vanish altogether, despite steady increases in the wealth of peasants, artisans, and shopkeepers.

For the first time, post–Black Death equality and inequality will be explored within three intersecting spheres: the economic, the political, and the cultural. While the economic has been the best studied, historians have yet to touch the cultural in terms of the prestige of non-elites and a paradoxical rise in cultural inequality. I will argue that the social-psychological needs of elites spurred by the Black Death and successive waves of plague spawned not only labour scarcities but also a consequential widening of political and cultural inequalities. One mechanism to enhance elites' ensuing social and psychological distinction was a sharp rise in the entry levels to commission artistic works in church buildings. These new needs for elite distinction transformed the underlying economic conditions for a new Renaissance patronage of art by the end of the fourteenth century. More than settling debates, this Element poses new questions and hypotheses to stimulate new research that will interlink economics, politics, and culture within the historical investigation of inequality.

Long-Term Trends in Inequality and Their Analysis

Questions of economic inequality were central to the analysis of political economy during the nineteenth century, especially in the classical works of David Ricardo (1772–1823) and Karl Marx (1818–83). During the last decades of the nineteenth century until after World War II, those concerns largely vanished from economic analysis until Simon Kuznets, future Nobel Prize–winner in economics (1901–85), published his groundbreaking article (Kuznets, 1955). Written in a period when Western economies were beginning to rebound from the war's destruction and misery, Kuznets presented a view that contrasted sharply with Ricardo and Marx. Economic inequality was not pictured as the evils of labour exploitation or the greed of industrial entrepreneurs. Rather, it was cast as an inevitability of economic growth and a positive indicator of prosperity across social classes. Further, his famous inverted-U trajectory (later known as the 'Kuznets curve') predicted an optimistic outcome – one, in fact, that had become evident in the West from the eve of World War I. While rapid economic growth with industrialization would drive inequality upwards – as in England in the eighteenth century, the Soviet Union in the 1930s, and the developing world after World War II – a second stage of diminishing inequality would soon follow.

The economic recession of 1973–5 spawned a period in which we still live, defying Kuznets' optimism. Yet economists and historians of equality failed to realize it until the recession of 2007–8. As late as 1995, in the first major historical study to investigate economic inequality before industrialization, Jan van Zanden, arguing on the basis of rental values of houses in the Low Countries, shored up Kuznets' model: since the late Middle Ages, inequality has been the consequence of economic growth. Furthermore, he went beyond Kuznets by positing a 'super-Kuznets curve' that spanned five centuries (van Zanden, 1995).

Shortly after the recession of 2007–9, a new generation of economic and social historians, trained in archival research and quantitative methods, began to question a principal plank of Kuznets' model of inequality as a function of economic growth. The most famous of these scholars has been Thomas Piketty. As with Kuznets' inequality, Piketty began with industrialization in the eighteenth century (Piketty, 2014). Between Kuznets and Piketty, other studies of inequality have linked the pre-industrial and industrial pasts, as in Jeffrey Williamson and Peter Lindert's study of the United States (Williamson & Lindert, 1980) and Şevket Pamuk's investigating inequality stretching through the Middle Ages and early modern period for Egypt and the Ottoman Empire (Pamuk, 2007). Most importantly, on the eve of Piketty's academic best-seller, Guido Alfani and his équipe at Bocconi University had already opened a new field of late medieval and early modern economic history by mapping long-term European inequality based on wealth and not income, reaching back to Europe's earliest tax registers (*estimi, castati, decime, cadastre*). For Tuscany and Piedmont, these survive from before the Black Death. Afterwards, especially during the sixteenth century, they became more abundant and fanned across the Italian peninsula and much of Europe (Alfani, 2015; Alfani & Ammannati, 2017).[3]

Two Types of Equality

Let us turn to the major conclusions drawn from the economic analysis of these pre-industrial fiscal records. First, scholars have calculated Gini coefficients, which estimate shifts in inequality of wealth, most often assessed from fiscal

---

[3] The project began in 2012 as a European Research Council STG-6 Research Grant: 'EINITE-Economic Inequality across Italy and Europe, 1300–1800'; www.dondena.unibocconi.it/EINITE.

records,[4] along with changes in the proportions of wealth calculated for various strata of populations. Despite problems of corruption, underestimation, and exemptions, trends in pre-industrial inequality show remarkably consistent patterns. From the mid-fifteenth or the beginning of the sixteenth century, depending on the place, inequality progressed steadily into the nineteenth century.[5] When national records across Europe and the Americas begin to appear in that century, the Gini coefficients connect almost seamlessly.[6] These pre-nineteenth-century results stretch across Europe and into the Middle East. Moreover, the rare reversals in mounting economic inequality were usually short-lived, as in northern Italy following the disastrous plagues of 1629–33, when Milan and Venice lost 30–50 per cent of their populations. The shift toward equality lasted less than a generation (Alfani & Murphy, 2017; Alfani & Percoco, 2019).

However, longer periods can be found. Another reversal from inexorable inequality ensued for Prato after its horrific siege and sack in 1512. Although given less attention in the literature, this reversal appears to have endured until a tax record (*decima*) in 1621 (Alfani & Ammannati, 2017: 1086–7). Other cities and their regions most likely experienced similar reversals after major sieges and sacks during the Italian wars (1494–1559), as with Brescia in 1512, Pavia in 1526–7, and Rome in 1527.[7] Trends in equality in these cities and their territories (perhaps because of the destruction of sources) have yet to be considered. However, this elongation of economic equality rested on economic conditions that appear to have differed from those following the Black Death. For more than a century, historians have emphasized the economic silver lining of the Black Death that gave rise to higher wages, greater productivity, better diets and housing, and new opportunities to purchase luxuries and enjoy leisure time (Dyer, 2002; Dyer, 2004; Gasquet, 1893: xvi; Goldthwaite, 1993; Hatcher, 1998: 70–1, 79–80; Herlihy, 1997; la Roncière, 1982; Le Roy Ladurie, 1966; and especially Stuart, 2006) for artisans across northern and central Italy. By contrast, with places destroyed by war, as in Prato and other regions in the sixteenth or seventeenth centuries, the equality that arose was one grounded in destitution that spread across social classes.

Second, against the Kuznets paradigm, the long pre-industrial period in inequality did not depend on economic growth. Instead, from the sixteenth

---

[4] Where 0 means perfect equality with each household or individual possessing the same income or wealth, and 1, complete inequality with one household or individual earning or owning everything.
[5] On the shortcomings of these records, see Alfani, 2010: 518, 524, and 537.
[6] Portugal is an exception but only after 1565; see Alfani, 2021: 14, based on Reis, 2017.
[7] For these sacks of cities, see Bowd, 2018; for ones in the countryside, Cohn, 2021.

century, inequality also grew steadily in periods and places with stagnating or declining economies, as in seventeenth- and eighteenth-century Italy. Third, as David Herlihy and Christiane Klapisch-Zuber demonstrated for Florentine Tuscany more than forty years ago, inequalities were greater in urban centres than in small towns or rural villages, and the larger the city, the higher the inequalities (Herlihy, 1967; Herlihy, 1968; Herlihy & Klapisch-Zuber, 1978). However, recent longer-term and European-wide studies of Alfani and his équipe have questioned whether those correlations can be generalized (Alfani, 2021).[8]

Finally, as claimed in our Preface, the most significant period when the gap between rich and poor narrowed was the post–Black Death century (either *c.*1350 to *c.*1450 or *c.*1375 to *c.*1475 or later, depending on place), as can be demonstrated quantitatively with fiscal sources. However, the character of that post–Black Death equality has yet to be explored, especially in its initial phases: was it one launched by growing prosperity of non-elites, or grounded in a levelling poverty across a wide spectrum of the population? Gini coefficients by themselves tell us little about these radically opposing economies.[9] For that, other quantitative evidence, such as real wages, has been beneficial.

From much more sketchy and problematic data,[10] Walter Scheidel, Steven Friesen, and Branko Milanovic have investigated an earlier and longer period of equality than that of the post–Black Death century. This was one which dominated the economic history of the Roman Empire and late Antiquity, from *c.*150 CE to 700. They have estimated that Roman economic inequality reached its peak around 150 CE. Then, for the next five and a half centuries, economic inequality declined through periods of economic and political expansion as well as contraction (Scheidel, 2017: 78–9; Scheidel and Friesen, 2009: 75–90)). The character of this equality, however, contrasts sharply with the economic experiences now argued for most of Western European during the late fourteenth and fifteenth centuries. For ancient Rome, rising living standards of non-elites did not underpin these years of equality. As Milanovic concluded, the transition was from a 'complex and prosperous but highly unequal society [to one that] became

---

[8] However, his first study of inequality from records of Ivrea (Alfani, 2010: 515, 527, and 545–6) emphasized the correlation between population size and inequality.

[9] Although Gini coefficients have been the standard statistic for evaluating levels of inequality since the early twentieth century, they have come under criticism mostly because of the inadequacy of a single figure for expressing varying differences in inequality across different social groups. Such has been the case with growing global inequality since the 1980s, where the startling rises in economic inequality have more sharply divided the middle classes from the rich and especially the super rich. As a result, economic historians such as Thomas Piketty (2020: 26–7) use stratified percentiles of wealth or income to chart inequality.

[10] Scheidel and Freisen (2009) admit: 'Our reconstruction is in its entirety a matter of controlled conjecture: undeniably conjecture, given the paucity of "hard" data' (63).

much poorer, primitive, and more equal' (Milanovic, 2019: 13; see also Alfani, 2021: 7).

Thus, declines in inequality following demographic disasters across time can manifest two opposing economic realities. For one, a sudden drastic shortage in the supply of labour increased labourers' bargaining powers and led to rising productivity, with peasants migrating to better lands, higher levels of capital investment, diversification of crops, and rising real wages in cities and the countryside. For the other, wars, sacks of cities, and long-term climatic deterioration 'levelled' populations (to use Scheidel's term), squeezing not only the poor but also middling groups and even some elites. In the post–Black Death century, both realities may have been at work at different phases of collapse, recovery, and transformation.

For instance, Prato may have experienced the longest period of post–Black Death equality that can be measured from successive tax records. From at least the *catasto* of 1428 (and probably before but yet to be calculated), Gini coefficients computed from fiscal records show equality on the rise until a tax record in 1621. However, the longevity of Prato's equality may rest in part on the rarity of fiscal surveys during the Medicean Grand Duchy, which provides only two snapshots, 1546 and 1621, after the last *catasto* of the Republican period in 1487.[11] Alfani and Ammannati consider that Prato's delay in conforming with the general sixteenth- and seventeenth-century trends of racing inequality 'could be partly the consequence of the terrible sack', but they hasten to add that Prato's shift to greater equality was already well underway before that disaster. They then list the city's Gini coefficients (0.683 in 1428, 0.624 in 1487, and 0.575 in 1546), as though behind these numbers lay much the same socio-economic factors suggestive of an equality grounded in prosperity, but without supplying supporting evidence (Alfani & Ammannati, 2017: 1086–7).

By its sack in 1512, and probably earlier in the Italian wars, Prato's equality had become one of hardship, economic decline, and poverty across social classes. Most likely, Prato's 'levelling' equality was already manifest by 1487, given what we know about Florentine domination over this subjugated town, reaching back to Medicean policies after 1434 and more so during the Laurentian period from the 1470s to 1492 (Petralia, 2000). Moreover, already by a tax record of 1393/4, the average wealth of Prato's propertied citizens was approaching that of mountain peasants north of the city: the mean family wealth in the city of Prato[12] was 283 *lire* versus 241 for the community of Morello, and

---

[11] It is assumed that the 1546 *decima* still reflected the consequences of the 1512 massacre. Sherer, 2017: 172, claims that 25–30 per cent of Prato's population was murdered.

[12] This analysis regards Prato's quarter of La Porta di Santa Trinita.

576 versus 446 if only property holders are tallied (Cohn, 1999: 61).[13] This similarity in wealth becomes striking when compared with city–countryside differences in 1427. Florentines were 8.5 times wealthier than those in market towns such as Empoli or San Gimignano, and 19.5 times wealthier than those in villages and 'sparsely populated areas' (calculated by Alfani & Di Tullio, 2019: 101, from data in Herlihy & Klapisch-Zuber, 1978). Of course, as Herlihy and Klapisch-Zuber demonstrated, Florentine wealth also exceeded that of residents from its six most populous subject cities (which included Prato) but by less (only three times).[14] Dividing by this factor, the average wealth of citizens in Prato would be expected to have been almost three times more than those residing in its *contado*. By contrast, Prato's average wealth was only 1.17 times more than its nearby mountaineers of Monte Morello, reflecting its relative poverty as an urban centre.

In addition, Prato's rising equality during the sixteenth century was probably not an outlier in Italy. If small towns and villages are included, hundreds of sacks destroyed Italian regions during the Italian wars, especially to 1530 (Bowd, 2018: 6, table I.1). In 1512 alone, two further massacres – Brescia and Ravenna – ranked among the most brutal in Italian history. Presently, no Gini coefficients or other markers of inequality have been calculated for either. Nor do fiscal data appear to have survived for major cities such as Milan that barely escaped terrible sacks.[15] Given chronicle descriptions of Milan's suffering from war, billeting of troops, and soaring taxation from 1499 to the 1530s, an equality of the levelling kind probably engulfed this capital city. Gianmarco Burigozzo, a Milanese shopkeeper whose chronicle stretched from 1500 to 1544, meticulously reported the billeting of and occupation by Spanish and German troops during these years. They destroyed Milanese homes and palaces, burnt their furnishings and squandered the resources of rich and poor alike. According to a wide variety of sources, this oppression, accompanied by excessive taxation, spurred mass migration of merchants, even noblemen, along with the poor.[16] Without doubt, these troops would have preferred their billets in palaces over hovels. Yet other than brief mentions of Prato, I know of no studies which explore the creation and persistence of this sixteenth-century

---

[13] From the fifteenth century, cities within the Florentine territory outside its *contado*, such as Poppi (Benadusi, 1996) or Pescia (Brown, 1982), did not begin to decline markedly until the late sixteenth or seventeenth century. Earlier, these towns benefited economically from their interdependence with Florence.

[14] Again, these calculations derive from Alfani and Di Tullio, 2019, taken from Herlihy and Klapisch-Zuber, 1978.

[15] For instance, in 1526, the supreme commander of the occupying German, Spanish, and Swiss troops in Lombardy, Antonio De Leyva, planned to sack the city; see Cohn, 2021.

[16] Burigozzo, *Cronica Milanese*, 67; and numerous references from Sanudo, *I diarii*; and other chronicles; see Cohn, 2021.

Italian equality grounded in poverty that stemmed from the carnage of the Italian wars.[17] Prato's post-1512 experience illustrates the problems of Gini coefficients for understanding trends in economic and social history. Beyond the obvious problems of fiscal data, this quantitative evidence can easily disguise diametrically opposed economic realities. More case studies, even ones from fragmented records as with Ivrea, need analysis and to be combined with narrative and other qualitative sources, especially for the post–Black Death century.

Equality and Inequality: The Importance of Qualitative Evidence

Reaching back more than fifty years, David Herlihy saw the necessity of combining quantitative with qualitative evidence to grasp economic and social change after the Black Death. In his study of the commune of Santa Maria Impruneta from the late thirteenth century into the third decade of the fifteenth century, he calculated Gini coefficients and plotted Lorenz curves[18] for the distribution of taxable wealth based on three tax surveys (*estimi*) in 1307, 1319, and 1330, plus the *catasto* of 1427. These showed the progressive march of wealth inequality in this large, predominantly rural community, fifteen kilometres south of Florence (Herlihy, 1968: 256–60). Recently, Alfani and Ammannati have questioned his analysis, maintaining that the Black Death marked a reversal towards more equal wealth distribution at Impruneta, along with Italy and across most of Europe, and this trend continued through most of the fifteenth century. They rightly charged that Herlihy had not standardized the wealth distribution for the earlier *estimi* when comparing it with the *catasto* of 1427, which listed those without taxable wealth. Moreover, with additional *estimi* for 1365 and 1402, a later *catasto* in 1458, and Florence's first *decima* in 1504, they added more observations for Impruneta (Alfani & Ammannati, 2017: 1082).

However, their critique failed to acknowledge fully Herlihy's qualitative analysis or his general conclusions. These presented a radical view on the *mezzadria* system (a variant of share-cropping). Herlihy's essay marked a departure from his mentor, Robert S. Lopez, who famously argued that the Black Death led to 'the economic depression of the Renaissance' (Lopez, 1953; Lopez & Miskimin, 1962). Herlihy showed that the *mezzadria* system spread

---

[17] One city to be studied with partial *estimi* (tax surveys) during the Italian wars (1487, 1518, and 1544) was Ivrea, where no growth in inequality occurred; instead, for a wealthier part of the city equality rose slightly; Alfani, 2010: 526.

[18] A graphic means to show levels of inequality, in which a 45-degrees diagonal line represents perfect equality.

dramatically from the late fourteenth century through the early fifteenth century in Impruneta and (in a later collaboration with Christiane Klapisch-Zuber) across more than a third of the Florentine state (Herlihy & Klapisch-Zuber, 1978: 268–86). During the late Middle Ages and Renaissance, this tenancy had not become the 'cruel' system of exploitation it would adopt a century later and that remained into the second half of the twentieth century. Instead, a new wave of urban investment in the land spawned agricultural improvements with increases in animal husbandry and diversification of crops. Vineyards and olive groves became interspersed with wheat and other grains. The *paesaggio* or agricultural organization and setting began to assume traits that continued into the twentieth century with mixtures of grains, olive groves, and vineyards in place of the previous near monoculture of wheat, ill-suited for Impruneta's hilly and rocky terrain. These improvements were not only more salubrious for the land, they also provided healthier diets and higher profits. In addition, the *mezzadria* system shielded rural labourers from Florence's burdensome taxation by categorizing them as '*nullatenenti*' – that is, possessing no property. As Herlihy made clear, on the books *mezzadri* appeared without any taxable wealth, but in terms of their calorific intake, increases in cattle, and healthier diets, the material conditions of Florence's peasantry improved vastly over those of the previously independent but impoverished *fictaioli*, who had owned their own plots. Herlihy concluded: 'The agricultural labourer, able to lease good farms on good terms with the aid of cheap capital, was better off than many of his forebearers. "Depression" with its connotations of unemployment, low wages or scarcity of capital does not describe his situation' (Herlihy, 1968: 276).[19] Moreover, for rural communes close to Florence's city walls, this post–Black Death investment in the land did not derive solely from Florentine elites. From nearly 1,000 surviving notarial land contracts redacted by the Mazzetti family of notaries between 1348 and 1426 in communities such as Santo Stefano in Pane and Sesto and up the hillsides of Monte Morello, Florentine shopkeepers and skilled artisans began investing in the land, purchasing small plots or even creating new farms (*poderi*) with *mezzadria* tenancies by the 1360s (Cohn, 1999: 18–19, 102–4, 108).

Herlihy attributed these changes in city and countryside to the transformative forces of the Black Death and subsequent plagues. His arguments did not

---

[19] Also, see Herlihy, 1967, for similar views on increases in animal husbandry, diminished demand for wheat, and 'much stronger demand for meat, wine, oil, and wood' (129); that the pre-Black Death agriculture had been 'destructive of the land and … of people too' (145); and that the *mezzadria* system was 'fairer to the land and to the people, [providing] Pistoia's Renaissance society with a firm and stable basis for its political life and cultural growth' (147). Moreover, Pistoia's urban economy recovered and expanded in the early fifteenth century by becoming 'more tightly integrated within a Tuscan regional economy' (178 and ch. 7).

depend solely on Gini coefficients. As he was well aware, the tax records had masked early fifteenth-century growth in rural wealth and prosperity. This view of the Black Death's silver lining for labour also held for Florence's urban population, as seen in his final, posthumous work (Herlihy, 1997: 47–51).[20] Yet, at the same time, he maintained that Tuscan societies during the fifteenth century were becoming more patrician and more unequal, both socially and politically. However, he never presented these trends as paradoxical or tried to reconcile them (Herlihy, 1967, chs. 8 and 9). Sections 2 and 3 of this Element will confront these paradoxes.

Finally, Herlihy and Klapisch-Zuber emphasized the growth of another sort of economic inequality in the Florentine state that stretched from the pre-Black Death period to at least the *Catasto* of 1427 (Herlihy, 1978; Herlihy & Klapisch-Zuber, 1978). This was an inequality between the city of Florence and its principal six cities and towns (Pisa, Pistoia, Arezzo, Prato, Volterra, and Cortona, all with populations above 3,000), its fifteen largest so-called 'villages' (places such as Empoli, San Gimignano, and Castiglion Fiorentino),[21] and then the myriad of real villages and hamlets. Alfani and his équipe investigated this economic inequality between cities and their *contadi* (Alfani & Di Tulio, 2019, 102–12), but not between capital cities and their subject towns and cities. The only historians to analyse this dimension of inequality are Herlihy and Klapisch-Zuber. Yet they examined it from one date alone – 1427. From that reference point, they speculated that Florence's great concentration of wealth ('a blazing sun of affluence surrounded by dim planets of wealth in small Tuscan cities and villages'; Herlihy & Klapisch-Zuber, 1978, 249) was of recent origins and stood in sharp contrast to Tuscany before the Black Death. Certainly from the perspective of the six major cities, this speculation appears correct. During the thirteenth through the early fourteenth century, all these cities had been vigorous centres of international commerce and banking, had possessed major cloth industries, or, as in the case of Pistoia, had been the major centre of Tuscany's iron works.

This subject of geographic inequality is ripe for new investigation across the early modern period and beyond Florence's hinterland. The local histories of Tuscan towns, such as Pescia in the Valdinievole and Poppi in the

---

[20] A decade later Herlihy changed his mind slightly on the *mezzadria* system and the Black Death's long-term silver lining. While he continued seeing it sustaining large families through good and bad times, he now emphasized the skewed distribution of wealth and constraints of indebtedness to their lords that limited economic incentives for peasants and artisans alike (Herlihy, 1978: 150–4).

[21] This was the Catasto's designation. They were, instead, market towns or what are now called 'quasi-città'(Pinto & Pirillo, 2013). Collectively, these comprised 25,000 inhabitants, nearly 10 per cent of the Tuscan population (Herlihy, 1978: 136).

Casentino, do not appear from qualitative evidence to map the 'monotonic' progression of inequality from the end of the fifteenth to the eighteenth century as emphasized by Alfani and his équipe for cities and towns in isolation, at least in their relationship to the capital, Florence. For Pescia and Poppi, the mid-sixteenth-century Medici opened new avenues for political and commercial symbiosis with Florence that provided new opportunities for local middlemen as intermediaries. The grand ducal aims led to the growth of a professional class of notaries and lawyers in these dependent towns, stimulated population growth and new investment in urban infrastructures and buildings, and changed patterns of consumption that reflected the needs of wealthier groups of inhabitants. Previously, in the fifteenth century, burdensome taxation from the capital had not only drained resources from these local economies; it also sparked mass migration that even threatened Florence's own economic and military objectives. By the seventeenth century, however, Medicean strategies of governance and economy shifted again. Florentine elites perceived provincial merchants, middlemen, and bureaucrats as competitors, and the Medici legislated crushing economic restrictions and impositions on them (Benadusi, 1996; Brown, 1982). Qualitatively, the early modern trend in Tuscan geographic inequality between the capital and some of its satellite towns appears as a 'V' and not the rising diagonal of inequality as observed for cities in isolation or from quantitative measures alone. Changes in regional inequality and equality now call for a new analysis with quantitative and qualitative testing.[22]

Prices and Wages

Despite numerous problems with price and wage data before the nineteenth century – matters of seasonal work, accompanying payments in kind, the weighting of 'baskets of basic consumables', credit and monies of account, small sample sizes, and more – these data can provide another key to gauge whether Gini coefficients at a given moment reflected rising economic prosperity for non-elites or an equality grounded in poverty over a wide spectrum of society.[23] As M.M. Postan argued for England, the first thirty years following the Black Death was a period of extreme dislocation: arable acreage decreased

---

[22] Such trends in geographic inequality do not contradict the general conclusions of Alfani and his colleagues: these contrasting trends could readily co-exist.

[23] Scheidel, 2017, sees all deviations from the normal increase of inequalities as resulting from exogenous shocks that negatively afflicted all social strata. For a critique of his pessimistic view, see Alfani, 2021: 38–40; and Piketty, 2020: 464. The Florentine historians cited hereafter were aware of these problems in their data. More trenchantly, Hatcher, 1998, 2013 and Hatcher and Stephenson, 2019 have criticized the limitations and misuse of wage and price data before the nineteenth century, especially by economists for comparisons from the thirteenth century to the

even more rapidly than the colossal drop in population (Postan, 1966: 570).[24] This paradoxical scarcity is reflected in prices for basic commodities, especially wheat. Although high across Europe on the eve of the Black Death, these prices continued to climb after populations plummeted in 1349, and rose again with further bouts of plague in 1374–5 (Herlihy, 1997: 47). At least one contemporary, the Florentine chronicler Matteo Villani, was aware of the paradox. On the eve of plague in 1363, he observed:

> It was thought that, given the lack of people, there ought to be a wealth of all the things, which the earth produces. On the contrary, through peoples' ingratitude unprecedented scarcity affected everything, and this continued for a long time. In certain lands ... there were severe and unprecedented famines. And again, it was thought that there ought to be wealth and abundance of clothing, and of all the other things that the human body needs ... but the opposite happened.[25]

However, most contemporaries, along with many modern historians, have failed to perceive or understand the paradox.[26] Contemporary citations of prices and nominal wages reflect this misunderstanding, especially during the first generation after the plague. For instance, the Florentine chronicler Marchionne di Coppo Stefani[27] and Giovanni Boccaccio (at least as regards gravediggers),[28] the English chronicler from Leicester, Henry Knighton,[29] the English poet William Langland,[30] the Latin poet John Gower,[31] and the Egyptian chronicler Maqrīzī[32] decried these high nominal wages, accusing labourers of cruel greed. As Siena's principal chronicler of 1348, Agnolo, the fat-so, proclaimed:

> those who survived attended to their own pleasures. Friars, priests, monks, the laity, and women all indulged in pleasures, indifferent to how much they spent or squandered. Everyone appeared as the rich ... no one knew how to wait for anything.[33]

---

present and for questions of standards of living and global divergences. Yet Hatcher, 1998, has used real wages to chart trends, even if not for absolute measures of standards of living.

[24] In addition, see Herlihy, 1964: 386; and Harriss, 1975: 322.

[25] Matteo Villani, *Cronica*, book I, ch. 5, cited in Herlihy, 1997: 46–7.

[26] See, for instance, Putnam, 1908. To the end of the twentieth century, prominent historians of medieval England praised her work as 'the definitive study' of labour legislation, despite her inability to recognize that rises in nominal wages after the Black Death did not necessarily constitute improvements in material conditions or that prices were rising faster than wages. On praise of Putnam by Rodney Hilton, Barry Dobson, John Hatcher, Steve Rigby, Mavis Mate, and David Farmer, see Cohn, 2007: 460.

[27] Stefani, *Cronica fiorentina*, 232.   [28] Boccaccio, *Decameron*, Day 1, Introduction, 15–16.

[29] Henry Knighton, *Chronicon*, 79.   [30] *Piers the Ploughman*, 89. See also Dyer, 2012: 44.

[31] Among other places, see Hatcher, 1998: 80, and his references.

[32] Maqrīzī, *Al-sulūk li-ma 'rifat duwal al-mulūk*, 380.

[33] Agnolo di Tura del Grasso, *Cronaca Senese*, 556.

Even Matteo Villani, who realized that the first fifteen years after the Black Death had yet to bless the poor or labourers with riches, nonetheless blamed them for their greed: 'And labour and the manufactures of every art and profession increased in disorderly fashion to double the price . . . '[34]

Historiographical interest in pre-industrial wages stretches back much longer than the recent enthusiasm for inequality studies. Instead of sprouting with the recession of 2007–8, prices and wage studies extend at least to James Thorold Rogers' first volume of *A History of Agriculture and Prices in England*, published in 1866. In *Das Kapital*, Karl Marx called it 'the first authentic "history of prices"'. Along with observations from the agronomist Arthur Young (1741–1820), comparing the 'pitiable' farmer in 1771 to 'his predecessor of the end of the fourteenth century', Marx followed Rogers' statistics to proclaim the fifteenth century as 'the golden age of the English labourer in town and country'.[35] Alfani has perceptively mentioned that Marx was possibly the first to provide 'an analysis of distributive dynamics in the very long run of history, from preindustrial to industrial times, arguing for increasing inequality' (Alfani, 2021: 21). Marx maintained that the well-being of English agricultural labourers declined absolutely from the fifteenth century to his own times.[36] Ever since, the historical analysis of prices and wages has been more or less continuous in the British Isles, with studies by Sir William Beveridge in the 1930s;[37] E.H. Phelps Brown and Sheila Hopkins in the 1950s; and David Farmer, Bruce Campbell and Mark Overton, Christopher Dyer, Robert C. Allen, Gregory Clark, and John Hatcher from the 1980s to 2019 (Allen, 2001; Campbell & Overton, 1993; Clark, 2007; Dyer, 1989 and 2002; Farmer, 1988; Hatcher, 2013 and Hatcher & Stephenson, 2019). For the twentieth century, French historiography has been equally rich in constructing price series and dividing them into long-term phases, which became an early hallmark of the *Annales* school with the work of Camille-Ernest Labrousse on the causes of the French Revolution (Labrousse, 1944) and, after the War, with *thèses d'État* that cut from the late Middle Ages to the twentieth century by Fernand Braudel, Pierre Chaunu, Jean Meuvret, René Baehrel, Pierre Goubert, and Emmanuel Le Roy Ladurie.[38]

---

[34] Matteo Villani, *Cronica*, Book I, ch. 5.
[35] Marx, *Capital*, I, 828. For criticism of this golden age, see Hatcher, 2013, and Hatcher and Stephenson, 2019.
[36] Marx, *Capital*, I, 896–913.
[37] On Beveridge and differences in his findings from Rogers', see Caferro, 2018:168.
[38] On the historiography of price and wage analyses, see Vigo, 1974, which begins with Adam Smith and compares England, France, and Italy.

By contrast, such work has gained less traction for pre-industrial Italy.[39] Studies before the end of World War II, such as Giuseppe Parenti's meticulous reconstructions and analysis of daily prices of various types of grain sold in Siena's Piazza del Campo, 1546 to 1765, and comparable work on early modern Florence seem to have been largely forgotten (Parenti, 1942 and 1939).[40] A recent work by the economic historian Mattia Fochesato (Bocconi University) raises big questions about the divergence of prices and wages between Mediterranean countries and the north of Europe from 1348 to the nineteenth century. His econometric analysis based on fourteen cities did not, however, engage in new archival digging. Instead, he relied on data previously assembled by Allen (2001) for thirteen of fourteen cities. Moreover, Allen had relied on earlier local studies that collected and assembled wage and price series mostly during the 1970s from various archives. Fochesato concludes from his regression analyses that 'all the European cities experienced the predicted Malthusian increase in real wages in the 14th–15th centuries, when large shocks reduced the population' (Fochesato, 2018: 104). Only during the sixteenth century did the north–south divide emerge, with four of his eight north-western cities escaping 'the Malthusian trap' (ibid., 110–11).[41] Yet his evidence on wages before the sixteenth century, particularly for southern Europe, is thin. For the six southern cities (Barcelona, Madrid, Valencia, Florence, Milan, and Naples), only Florence provides observations for the fourteenth century, and only one other city – Valencia – supplies data before 1500 (ibid., 113). In Italy, Naples' wage data begins only in 1548, and Milan's in the seventeenth century (ibid., 111–14). In short, for the convergence of north and south in the fifteenth century when all of Europe had supposedly been locked in a post–Black Death 'Malthusian trap', not only does Florence stand for all of Italy, it stands for all of southern Europe.

---

[39] According to Vigo, 1974, no data was known for constructing real wage series in Italy before the fifteenth century. The best ones he located were from masons in Vigevano, 35 kilometres southwest of Milan, which begin in 1411. He compares these with one datapoint from Milan, taken from its cathedral works in 1391, and predicts that Italian wage trends took off around 1400 (384, 387–8, and table 1, 396).

[40] For instance, Fochesato, 2018, focusing on medieval and early modern prices and wages and citing 204 references, does not mention Parenti. Nor did Allen, 2001, know about the Sienese data; he instead invented the more problematic combination of Florentine wages for the late Middle Ages and Renaissance fused with Milan's in the eighteenth century as though they were the same place. Fochesato then adopted the same. Tognetti, 1995: 263, notes Parenti's work but makes no use of it.

[41] The first usage of 'Malthusian trap' that I have found comes from North and Thomas, 1973: 69, and has found a recent revival: see Fochesato, 2018: 95, 104, 109, and 111. The trap was the supposed pre-industrial mechanism, whereby resources rise arithmetically, while populations increase exponentially. For a critique of long-term changes and divergences in wages, see Caferro, 2018: 180–6.

Of course, economists and other social scientists regularly utilize archival materials for advanced analysis previously collected by historians. The question is: why has so little material been published by Italianists on price and wage data before 1500? Florence presently stands out as the lone beacon of price and wage studies.[42] For late medieval and Renaissance Italy, I know of only two studies that venture beyond its city walls to analyse the effects of the Black Death on wages, and both concern cities subject to Florentine rule.[43]. However, as far as hospital and confraternal records go – the principal repositories of price and wage series – Florence's archival sources are hardly unique for the fourteenth or fifteenth centuries.[44]

At least seven historians – Giuliano Pinto, Richard Goldthwaite, Charles-M. de la Roncière, Christiane Klapisch-Zuber, Franco Franceschi, Sergio Tognetti, and William Caferro – have assembled wage and price series from various monastic, hospital, municipal, and private account books (*ricordi*). Forty years ago, Richard Goldthwaite signalled the possibilities of constructing such indices across late medieval and early modern Italy (Goldthwaite, 1980). Five years earlier, he had completed his study of grain prices in Florence, based primarily on the hospital account books of Santa Maria Nuova and with an eye to investigate real wages in the building trades (Goldthwaite, 1975). At same time, Giuliano Pinto had constructed a 'budget-type' for wet-nurses and other wage earners employed by the hospital of San Gallo, but only for eleven years: 1395 to 1406 (Pinto, 1974). Later, with other sources, he extended his analysis for a wider body of workers from 1380 to 1430 (Pinto, 1981). In the 1970s, Charles-M. de la Roncière was completing his five-volume *thèse d'État* on Florentine prices and wages from the end of the thirteenth century to 1380, only part of which he later transformed into an 877-page book (la Roncière, 1976 and 1982). Like Goldthwaite, his wage data centred on the building trades. From Florence's central hospital, however, la Roncière also included wages of cobblers and gardeners (*ortolani*) in the city and the countryside. As importantly, he broadened the range of data on consumption with different types of cereals, olive oil, wine, varieties of vegetables, meats, eggs, fruit, wood, and more (la Roncière, 1976 and 1982). Sergio Tognetti continued this work by summarizing the above-mentioned studies and adding new price data from other ecclesiastic

---

[42] See Vigo, 1974. Moreover, Tognetti, 1995: 273–4, 276, placed the Florentine trends in larger contexts by turning to England, Germany, Spain, and France; yet he mentions none from any other Italian region. The same goes for la Roncière, 1982: 755–7.

[43] One was for Prato, incorporated into Florence's *contado* in 1351 (Pinelli, 1999); the other, for Pisa, was incorporated into the Florentine state in 1406 (Casini, 1983). By the sixteenth century, this Italian coverage changes; see for instance Zanetti, 1964; and Damsholt, 1964.

[44] Such material is not available for every city-state. Herlihy, 1967: 150, could find only sporadic references to wages in late medieval Pistoia.

records that extended la Roncière's research to the end of the fifteenth century (Tognetti, 1995).

In addition, Pinto, la Roncière, and Tognetti constructed new 'budget-types' or 'baskets of consumables' and discovered trends that varied from those based on grain prices alone, especially for more expensive items that had become more prominent in non-elite diets during the fifteenth century. Moreover, Florence may be the only place in Europe to possess a contemporary calculation of an index of spending before the nineteenth century. To argue for fiscal reform around 1445, the bureaucrat Lodovico Ghetti calculated a 'budget-type' of private expenditures from records of consumption. Goldthwaite, la Roncière, and Tognetti used Ghetti's model and compared it with Pinto's,[45] but surprisingly historians have yet to employ these models mathematically to estimate real wages over time (Goldthwaite, 1980: 438–9; and Tognetti, 1995: 308–9). Instead, to calibrate real wages (which remains rare in these studies), they reverted to depending on wheat prices only.

The Character of Post–Black Death Equality: An Open Question

Regarding shifts in non-elite prosperity that buttressed opposing types of equality wrought by the plagues, the wages presented by Florentine scholars suggest conflicting scenarios. First, neither Klapisch-Zuber nor Pinto concentrated on the first thirty years after the Black Death. Nonetheless, Klapisch-Zuber concluded that only by 'the first half of the fifteenth century' had 'salaries paid to female servants' reflected 'the demographic and economic factors [that] favored them'. With their apex at mid-century, these real wages (based on grain prices taken from Goldthwaite) more than doubled from what they had been in 1348 (Klapisch-Zuber, 1986: 65–6). She declared the fifteenth century 'a golden age for female servants' that ended by 1500, when wet-nurses earned only a quarter of the rates they had in 1420–70 (ibid., 63).[46] For calculating real wages of agricultural workers and unskilled (*manovali*) and skilled workers (*maestri*) in the building industry from 1380 to 1430, Pinto was more cautious, calling for new research. Yet his table of real wages parallels the trends found by

---

[45] Pinto, 1974:158, from records of San Gallo, 1395–1406, hypothesized that 50 per cent of labourers' budgets were spent on food (*alimentare*), 25 per cent on wine, 15 per cent on meat, 5 per cent on olive oil, and 5 per cent on cooking fuel. For another hypothetical model, see la Roncière, 1982. Goldthwaite, 1980, examining Ghetti's model, concluded: 'food was by far the most expensive item in the household budget of the working man' (347). Goldthwaite has been the only one of these scholars to estimate rent within the 'budget-type' (ibid., 344–50). See also Tognetti, 1995: 288–9, 309; and la Roncière, 1982: 753–4.

[46] See also Pinto, 1974: 152, 157, 160–1, which compares wages of masons, wet nurses, messengers, heralds, bell-ringers, cooks, and other servants ('donzelli') in the Florentine government (*Signoria*), calculated in kilogrammes of grain and caloric values; and Sandri, 1991: 97.

Klapisch-Zuber: not until the 1420s – more than sixty years after the Black Death – did wages begin to rise significantly (Pinto, 1981).[47]

In his 1975 article on grain prices, Goldthwaite, without yet calculating real wages in the building trade, hypothesized that wages began increasing only at the end of the fourteenth or beginning of the fifteenth century.[48] Five years later, however, armed with real wages calculated in *staia* (bushels) of wheat, he changed his mind:

> The dramatic rise in nominal wages after 1348 brought an immediate gain in the worker's real wages ... By 1360, when prices began to level off, the worker's earning power had increased by 50 percent over what it had been before 1348 ... In short, from the Black Death to the end of the fifteenth century wages were significantly higher than they had been previously, with a particularly high plateau stretching over the first two-thirds of the fifteenth century ... The improvement of the Florentine worker's standard of living immediately after 1348 is notable. (Goldthwaite, 1980: 334–5)

His later statistical overview was, however, less scrupulous than his qualitative discussions on the limitations of evaluating wages from the building industry alone. Because of seasonal fluctuations, short-term employment, and fewer days of work, higher wages were necessitated in this industry than in others (ibid., 331).[49] First, without explanation, Goldthwaite calculated the real wages of unskilled workers (*manovali*) only, although he had also collected nominal wages for skilled builders, and these workers comprised 'well over one-half of the labor force in construction' (Goldthwaite, 1980: 348–9). More to our point: his data fail to support his claims of workers' increased prosperity during the second half of the fourteenth century. Goldthwaite's records allowed him to present only a few datapoints before 1380, and, before the Black Death, only one year (1310). His next datapoint for real wages does not appear until 1364, fifty-five years later and sixteen years after the Black Death. In addition, before 1371, he presents further data for one year alone (1365). Only from 1380 does his data begin to trace a more continuous trend, with nine missing years before 1400, then with only eight missing years for the fifteenth century. Therefore, no matter what the values of these data, claims of real wages rising immediately after the Black Death are questionable.

---

[47] Pinto, 1981: 187 and 178: these wages, calculated in weights of grain, increased only by 7 per cent, 1380–83 to 1421, and 1384 to 1393 and 1408 to 1412; real wages fell by 34 per cent and 18 per cent, respectively.

[48] Goldthwaite, 1975: 20 ('fino del Trecento') and 16 ('L'aumento fu invece sostanziale dopo il 1400').

[49] He was also aware of the limitations of generalizing from wheat prices alone. Others have pointed to the discrepancies between relying on wholesale grain and bread prices; see Vigo, 1974: 380; and Allen, 2001: 419–20.

As William Caferro has recently claimed, Goldthwaite was not alone in claiming that wages soared immediately after the Black Death. Rather, based on Florence's wage data, gathered almost exclusively from religious institutions, this position has become the orthodoxy. Following in Pinto's footsteps for a later period, Caferro ventured outside religious institutions to locate and analyse wage data for the years immediately after the Black Death, 1349–50, and in an epilogue, 1345 to 1354 (Caferro, 2018).[50] Various archives of the Florentine state list numerous wage payments to officials, soldiers, and artisans involved in military missions, such as Florence's defence of Scarperia in 1349–50. In fact, Caferro compiled far more wage statistics for these years than from all the religious institutions thus far mined for the Florence state for the entire fourteenth century. Instead of confirming the consensus, Caferro exposed the great complexity and enigmas presented by these data: the diversity of payments in silver, gold, and monies of account; non-monetized emoluments in food, clothes, gratuities, and bonuses; and the importance of social status as a determinant of wages.[51] He concentrated, for instance, on the differences between the wage rates of the cavalry and castellans on the one hand and the infantry on the other. While the nominal wages of the infantry rose from 1349 to 1350 along the lines outlined by Goldthwaite and la Roncière for the lesser-skilled in the building industry and gardeners, those of the cavalry did not change, and for the more prestigious castellans they either remained stable or fell. Next, across a wide range of government employees – town criers, bell-ringers, cooks, various ranks of the police, musicians, and messengers – Caferro found that their wages mostly failed to increase in 1349–50. Caferro's wage data confounds any unified story. Instead, they present various and contradictory trajectories that fail to abide with the supply of labour drastically diminished by the Black Death (Caferro, 2018: chs. 3–5). Overall, his research shows a fall in wages immediately after the Black Death, and these are nominal wages. Based on previous research of basic prices of commodities in these two years, the purchasing power of these wages points to dramatic decline.

Before 1380, a story of consistent and soaring wages propelled by the Black Death as calculated by real wages becomes even more questionable. Despite the mammoth research of la Roncière, especially regarding the wide diversity of food prices that show a variety of trajectories and 'baskets' of expenditures for

---

[50] Franceschi, 1993, is an exception. However, his data begins only in the 1360s, and mainly after the defeat of the Government of the Minor Guilds in 1382.

[51] To this list, Caracausi (2018) has added further determinants of wages for early modern Italy, such as the age of the worker, civil status, work experience, reputation, whether hazardous tasks were involved, and skills. Instead of the dichotomy of skilled and unskilled, a continuum of skill levels determined wages.

labourers, he curiously avoided presenting any real wages, even those calculated from wheat prices. Instead, such estimates rely on Goldthwaite's wages for the unskilled in construction alone in terms of bushels of wheat. First, for these years, the economic downturn and famine described by Matteo Villani in 1353 and 1357 do not appear in Goldthwaite's tables, and, by 1371, wages in bushels (0.35) had declined by more than half their value in 1364 or 1365 (0.79 for both years), returning almost exactly to the single pre-Black-Death point of 0.31 bushels in 1310. With the years of food shortages and plague in 1374 and 1375, real wages plunged further: in 1374 to two-thirds what they had fetched before the Black Death (0.21 bushels) and, in the following year, to only half of what these labourers earned before the Black Death (0.16 bushels). These real wages were the lowest of any calculated by Goldthwaite until 1527 (0.15) and were equal to the years during the eight-and-a-half-month siege of Florence in 1529–30. Nor did real wages recover rapidly after 1374–5. In 1376 (at 0.33), they approximated the value in 1310, and after 1364–5, the rate was not surpassed until 1424 (Goldthwaite, 1980: appendix three, 438–9). As with the domestics analysed by Klapisch-Zuber, the period of mounting prosperity for Florence's unskilled construction workers began only in the fifteenth century.

More dramatic was the decline in wages assessed by Franco Franceschi for workers in Florence's largest industry in the fourteenth century: woollens. Nominal wages and rates for piece-work for apprentices to skilled dyers declined from the Revolt of the Ciompi (1378) into the fifteenth century by between 5 and 25 percent. Here, the usual 'stickiness' of nominal wages (see note 103) did not prevail. Because of the drop in the prices of necessities, however, workers even in this declining industry eventually appear better off, but not until the second decade of the fifteenth century (Franceschi, 1993: tables 23 A–F, 24 and 25; 242–8, 263–5, and 330–3).

Unlike Goldthwaite, la Roncière paid much greater attention to these sharp variations in prices and therefore to the wages and the well-being of skilled and unskilled workers during the first generation after the Black Death. Moreover, his work is steeped in greater data collection of prices pertaining to many more foodstuffs and necessities, such as firewood. Although the building trades provide the backbone of his wage series, he collected figures for other workers, including some for woolworkers. For la Roncière, two economic 'époques' appear during the first generation after the Black Death: one of rising nominal wages, 1361–9; the other, of crisis, 1370–7 (la Roncière, 1982: 458).[52] Yet his final conclusion undermines his earlier, more nuanced view and returns to

---

[52] Shortly thereafter, he stretches the first period back to 1350, apparently forgetting about the famines of 1353 and 1357 and failing to support his claim with estimates of real wages.

a more simplistic, neo-Malthusian picture of immediate and long-term change with the Black Death: 'after 1350 Florentine wages reflected the scarcity of labourers that characterized the West' (ibid., 769). In addition, none of his numerous tables, graphs, appendices, and descriptions of prices chart any real wages or discuss what basket of goods he had used to construct such a table.[53] Finally, Tognetti's excellent synthesis of Pinto, Goldthwaite, and la Roncière, accompanied by his new price data, first supports Goldthwaite's but ultimately Klapisch's conclusions (although he never cites her): 'the trends in prices and wages show that the two decades following the plague and the first seventy years of the fifteenth century were, without doubt, the two epochs that favoured the wellbeing of the *popolo minuto*, but the second period was the most important' (Tognetti, 1995: 275).

Back to my earlier hypothesis: the data on prices and wages distilled from these voluminous studies strongly suggest that the equality of the post–Black Death century or more (1350 to 1475 or later) does not chart one sort of equality. Rather, the decline in inequality as measured by Gini coefficients during the first fifty years after the Black Death reflects more an equality grounded in poverty as opposed to one propelled by non-elite prosperity (except for the decade of the 1360s). But by the fifteenth century that equality had transformed into what historians lodged in neo-Malthusian logic have assumed arose immediately after 1348: equality driven by the supply of and demand for labour

Another Use of Tax Records

So, can historians go further in determining the character of equality for the first generation or longer after the Black Death? Did different sectors and places chart different trajectories even within the Florentine state? Sources for this question have a long tradition of analysis that preceded World War II. Here, Florence certainly was not unique in terms of its surviving archival sources.[54] These sources regard property values assessed in *estimi*, *catasti*, or *decime*. These plot many more points before the Black Death and through the 1380s than are presently available from calculations of real wages. Second, they allow more detailed analysis beyond cities. Third, the historian can compare changes over time without relying predominantly on a single trade – the building

---

[53] His chart 54 (703) compares prices in silver, wages of masons in silver, and population wages and population figures, but not wages in terms of any expenditures. Without explanation, these increase sharply in 1348 and level off in 1350, then are without variation until the end of his analysis in 1380 – that is, through the good times of the 1360s and bad times of the 1370s.

[54] For Piedmont, see Alfani, 2015; for the Veneto, Alfani and Di Tullio, 2019; and for the *contado* of Lucca, particularly the *Sei miglia*, Leverotti, 1992; and Ammannati, 2015: 21–45, with *estimi* in 1331–2, 1333–5 (additions), 1367–8, 1383, 1411–13, and more for the fifteenth century to 1561.

industry – with its peculiarities of seasonality and short-term employment. Finally, and most importantly, in evaluating trends in prosperity from these records, historians can reach beyond the present Florentine-centricity to examine more regions in central and northern Italy. Florence no longer needs to stand for all of southern Europe before 1500.

To be sure, the usual problems with fiscal records remain: personal exemptions, underreporting, and corruption. Yet these problems, I assert, are less extreme with calculations of changes in the wealth of labourers or non-elites over time than relying on Gini coefficients for trends in inequality from these same documents. The latter depends on cross-class comparisons, in which elites possessed strikingly different powers compared with non-elites to manipulate their taxable wealth, as is well attested in petitions and tax revolts across medieval and early modern Italian history (Cohn, 1999; 2006; 2021).

The survey and analysis of these documents could easily constitute a major research project comparable to Alfani's at the Bocconi. However, by examining *estimi* for the *contado* of Florence, north of the city to the Apennine border with Bologna, I previously tracked changes in wealth from 1356 to 1487 using ten *estimi* and *catasti* with ten-year intervals or less until 1412. None of these communities – in plains, hills, mountains, or the city of Prato – registered a leap forward in prosperity for non-elites immediately after the Black Death, whether calculated with or without the propertyless. As with Klapisch-Zuber's calculation for *balìa* or John Munro's for the Low Countries (Munro, 2003), the take-off in wealth of those residing in mountainous zones begins only in the fifteenth century, and probably not until the second decade of that century. However, prosperity for those in the plains near the city of Florence begins as early as 1365 (Figures 1–3) Given that this region of the plains included places, such as Sesto, with post-plague populations of more than a thousand and that were more tightly integrated within the urban economy of Florence than distant and more independent mountain communities of the Alpi Fiorentine, trends in wealth in the plains probably paralleled those residing in Florence more closely. Because of Florence's power to place all direct taxation onto its countryside, except for three times between 1315 and the Catasto of 1427, the city of Florence becomes greatly diminished in this analysis. This did not, however, occur for many other late medieval and Renaissance Italian cities, which now cry out for construction of similar trajectories of non-elite wealth over the post–Black Death century.

This section has called for new research beyond Florence to calculate and compare economic trajectories of equality and prosperity of non-elites within Italian city-states from the Black Death to the sixteenth century. For the

The Renaissance

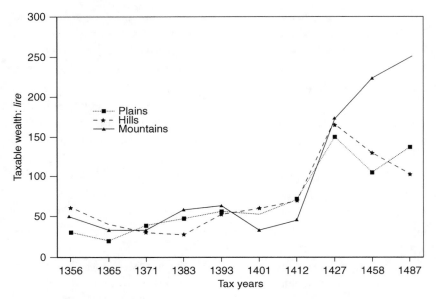

Figure 1 Wealth, Including the Propertyless: Mountains, Hills, and Plains.

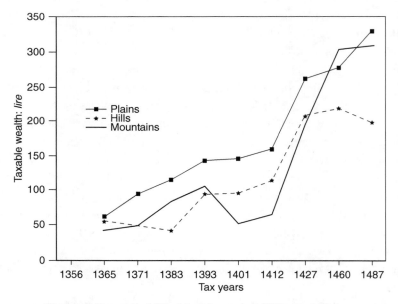

Figure 2 Propertied Wealth: Mountains, Hills, and Plains.

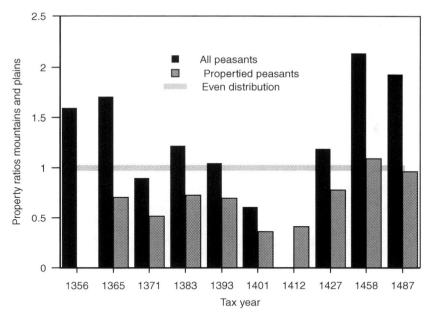

Figure 3 Wealth Ratios: Mountains vs. Plains.

moment, and for the purposes of the next two sections, I hypothesize that rising economic equality after the Black Death presented two opposing economic realities. For places such as the mountain communities north of Florence, the equality of the first half-century following the Black Death was a 'levelling' one, grounded in declining prosperity across social classes that at times created famine conditions.[55] For communities in the plains near Florence, however, the switch to an equality based in prosperity appeared earlier, in the 1360s. For the city of Florence, taken from the limited data on real wages, the 1360s also appears to have been a switch to prosperity, even if it lasted less than a decade. The steadier and more pronounced trends had to await the fifteenth century. Moreover, none of these places support the assumed Malthusian logic that the Black Death's sudden creation of labour scarcity immediately propelled non-elites, and especially those of the lower echelons, into prosperity. These economic considerations are important for understanding trends reflected from quantitative and qualitative evidence in the following two sections, when shifts in politics and culture took crucial but contrary paths to those seen in the economy.

---

[55] On taxable wealth and qualitative evidence of economic and ecological decline in these mountains to *c.*1412, see Cohn, 1999, ch. 2.

2 The Paradox of Political Inequality

The aftermath of Europe's most catastrophic demographic event, the Black Death of 1347–51, contributed to a rare occurrence in Western civilization. Afterwards, for a century or more, the gap between rich and poor narrowed. As explored in the previous section, this switch to decreasing inequality began in most places with the Black Death and where tax records survive can be seen across Europe, in cities and the countryside, and across radically different political regimes: guild-controlled city-states, oligarchies, and monarchies. There were, however, exceptions, such as with cities in Piedmont (Sabaudian State), where the inequality decline began early in the fourteenth century and continued, as for many other places, into the 1470s (Alfani, 2021: 11; Alfani, 2015). Towns in the Venetian Republic present further exceptions, as with Bergamo's decline in inequality from 1555 until sometime between two tax records of 1640 and 1704. More dramatic were trends in Verona, which reflect almost the opposite of the general pattern. From its earliest *estimo* in 1409, instead of equality reigning, inequality rises to 1456. Then equality takes over, with Gini coefficients descending for the next 150 years or more. The start of the inequality regime here is marked only by its tax record of 1696. Explanations for these exceptions have yet to be addressed by Alfani, or anyone else.[56]

At the later end of the spectrum, reversals that initiated the long history of inequalities lasting to the eve of the First World War with only brief intermissions[57] show less consistency than for the beginnings of the post–Black Death reign of equality. For some the switch to inequalities began around 1450, but for others it had a bumpier ride, as with Bergamo, or a contrary one, as with Verona. Moreover, for Flanders and Brabant, based on eighteen cities and towns, inequalities remained stagnant or declined throughout the seventeenth century (Alfani & Ryckbosch, 2016: 143–53, chart on 146). By contrast, Poggibonsi, north of Siena, began its march of inequality at the end of the fourteenth century (Alfani & Ammannati, 2017: 1079).

As examined in the previous section, trends of non-elite prosperity after the Black Death were less consistent across Europe than measures of inequality. While prosperity may have accompanied the sharp fall in the supply of labour in 1348 in some places, it was certainly not universal as economic historians such as Allen and Fochesato have assumed (Fochesato, 2018). Instead, historians have argued that the turning point for England emerged only around 1375 or after the English Uprising of 1381 (Hilton, 1973). According to Christopher

---

[56] See Alfani and Di Tullio, 2019: 96–9, 105, and 186.
[57] On the short-term impact of the 1629–33 plagues and comparison with 1348 on inequality, see Alfani and Murphy, 2017: 314–34; 318–19, 322–3, 335; and Alfani and Percoco, 2019.

Dyer, in 1375 'a new era of cheap and plentiful food' arose, marking an end of 'hunger-driven mortality' (Dyer, 1998: 70). For the Low Countries, the transition did not take place until the fifteenth century (Munro, 2003), and the same can be said from fiscal assessments of wealth for many villages within the *contado* of Florence. As seen in Section 1 with Florence, the path to increased prosperity before the fifteenth century could vary from one profession or a range of skills to another.

Economists and economic historians have yet to study, and few have even recognized, the variety in these trends before the north–south divergence of the sixteenth to eighteenth centuries. Instead, they have explained the supposed general improvements in wages (nominal and real) after the Black Death across Europe, north and south, as resulting from a 'Malthusian Trap'[58] created by the dramatic shift in the supply of labour. Yet, because of endogenous factors such as fertility rates and taxation and exogenous ones such as warfare, the demographic trends from the fourteenth to the sixteenth centuries were not always the same across Europe. In Normandy, for instance, plague, the Hundred Years' War, and brigandage reduced towns and countryside to what Guy Bois called a medieval 'Hiroshima' (Bois, 1976). By contrast, no marauding troops invaded the hinterland of Canterbury, destroying villages, wrecking harvests for a generation or more, or reducing its major city to starvation, such as happened to Rouen in 1418–19.[59]

In addition, demographic recovery rates of cities and regions from the Black Death and successive bouts of plague have shown sharp differences. England did not surpass its pre-Black Death population until well into the eighteenth century. This demographic brake has led economists and historians to argue that the delay was a major reason for British labourers not to suffer severe declines in wages or standards of living from the sixteenth to the nineteenth centuries such as was witnessed on the continent, except in the Low Countries (Allen, 2001: 413, 417, 429, 434–5, which relies on de Vries, 1984; and Pamuk, 2007: 294 and 308). But high wages cannot be associated everywhere with low population recovery. One place to suffer wage declines as steep as anywhere in these centuries was Florence, but its population did not reach pre-Black-Death levels until after unification in the 1860s, (Malanima, 2013: 55).[60] Moreover, some towns in its territory, such as San Gimignano and Santa Maria Impruneta, still have not

---

[58] See Section 1, note 41.

[59] *Mémoires de Pierre de Fenin*, 104; and Bois, 1976. For demographic developments in Canterbury, see Hatcher, 1986.

[60] Florence's failure to recover demographically cannot be pinned on the devastating plagues of the seventeenth century. Unlike Milan, Venice, Genoa, Palermo, Naples, and many smaller towns in these regions with population losses of between 33 per cent and 65 per cent, Florence lost just 12 per cent in its only seventeenth-century plague, that of 1630–3; Henderson, 2020: 42.

recovered their pre-plague populations. Scholars have yet to compare different end points of the equality century for different cities and regions to understand the causes or the consequences of these differences.

Trajectories in Personal Freedom

More importantly, the growth in economic equality after the Black Death had consequences beyond economics, and these remain largely unexplored. First, they concern personal freedoms and the status of peasants across wide tracts of Europe. Against roughly similar demographic changes wrought by plague, radically different outcomes could ensue, thereby defying a simple demographic determinism. Most notable of the post–Black Death consequences for rural labour was the long-recognized divide between Eastern and Western Europe. In most regions of Western Europe various forms of serfdom had disappeared, even if the decline had begun two or more centuries earlier. The consequences for regions of Eastern European and even in parts of Germany ran against supposed Malthusian notions of the supply and demand of labour. Serfdom increased and became more restrictive. In places, it resembled slavery with body serfdom, when attachment to the land changed to that of the lord. This stark division in the consequences of peasant freedom provided a key component in Robert Brenner's famous essay attacking the neo-Malthusian arguments of the 1950s and 1960s (Aston & Philpin, 1985; and Brenner, 1976).[61]

However, historians of eastern Europe have shown that these differences in late fourteenth- and fifteenth-century developments of land tenure and peasant status have been exaggerated, especially before the seventeenth century. For Bohemia, for instance, John Klassen argued that the status of peasants on some large estates had improved or remained much the same from 1380 to 1433 (Klassen, 1990: 257 and 268). More fundamentally, Heide Wunder accused Brenner of falling victim to 'the Prussian myth' of two types of post-plague developments in labour and land tenure: one for west of the Elbe (river), the other for the east. Instead, large regions, such as Prussia, where the crown protected the peasantry, contradicted Brenner's simple divide (Wunder, 1978).[62] However, her more complex and variegated picture of peasant status east of the Elbe in fact supports Brenner's central thesis: the neo-Malthusian demographic model and notions of the supply of labour fail to account for the

---

[61] The principal protagonists of the neo-Malthusian arguments were Postan on English agrarian history, and Le Roy Ladurie, 1966, for France. For references to Postan, see Brenner, 1976.

[62] Also, see Postan and Hatcher, 1978: 27: 'the rise of serfdom beyond the Elbe largely post-dates the late-medieval fall in population ... spreading widest in the sixteenth and seventeenth centuries and culminating in rather different circumstances in eighteenth-century Russia'.

multiplicity of developments in peasant power and liberties after the Black Death in Western as well as Eastern Europe.

Moreover, in Western Europe, the Black Death did not spell progress in personal and contractual freedoms everywhere. In post–Black Death Denmark, for instance, aggressive actions by its nobility quickly and successfully countered the initial post-plague opportunities of peasants improving their legal status and extending political rights (Orrman, 2003). More contentious has been the case of England from the Black Death to the Uprising of 1381: did the Black Death spur a 'feudal reaction' with harsher forms of serfdom? The debate has weighed heavily on the significance of the 1381 Uprising. One argument has held that English landlords, armed with new wage legislation and administrative structures of the Justices of the Peace, successfully combated the sudden shift in the supply and demand for labour that favoured workers. Similar to the nobility in some regions east of the Elbe, English landlords turned the clock back as far as personal freedoms went. Harsher forms of servitude restricted peasant mobility and diminished their rights for a generation following the Black Death. However, around the time of the so-called English Peasants' Revolt of 1381,[63] the economic well-being and the political, juridical, and social status of the peasantry began to shift. England no longer went the way of the East; market mechanisms undermined coercive labour laws: and land tenure shifted from servitude to economic rents.[64] By the 1420s most manorial demesnes had been leased out and mechanisms for controlling rural labour had declined, as eloquently testified in the sharp decline in the number of cases landlords could bring before their manorial courts (Dyer, 2004: 146–7).

However, since publication of Mark Bailey's meticulous research on the chronology of the decline of serfdom over large parts of England after the Black Death to the mid-sixteenth century, that picture of English 'feudal reaction' has been questioned, even if the significance of the 1381 Uprising has not been overturned. From a sample of thirty-eight manors across different species of landlords and regions in England, Bailey challenged the traditional view that the decay of serfdom (villeinage) had to await the 1370s or later. Instead, these coercive tenures were already in retreat from the 1350s and had largely disappeared by the 1380s 'on all types of manors' (Bailey, 2014, cited on p. 287; also see 289–306, and 310).

---

[63] In addition to revolts in 1381 occurring in numerous cities and towns – London, York, St Albans, Winchester, etc. – those marching into London in early June partially came from small towns such as Ware; see Prescott, 1984.

[64] On this trajectory, see most prominently Hilton, 1973, ch. 5.

Curiously, these European debates on post-plague trajectories of rural labourers' freedoms have hardy figured in recent Italian historiography. As with east
of the Elbe, Italy comprised a wide spectrum of tenurial relations with various
forms of free labourers bound only by rents and taxes, while other agricultural
workers, called 'vassals', were subject to powerful heads of small feudal states
in Alpine regions,[65] and in southern Italy were subject to lords of *latifundia*
(Bresc, 1986). Moreover, such 'feudal' survivals are found in the Apennines
within the northern and northeastern boundaries of Florentine Tuscany (Cohn,
1999). However, the most prevalent agrarian change over the post–Black Death
century, at least in Tuscany, was the growth of the *mezzadria* system, despite its
earliest surviving document originating in 821 (Imberciadori, 1951: 18 and 37).
As reviewed in Section 1, Black Death economics spurred urban merchants and
even artisans to invest in agriculture, and these investments benefited the land,
productivity, and well-being of rural toilers. As Herlihy and Klapisch-Zuber
have argued, over-cultivation of grain and excessive taxation by the city had
pushed peasants in Florentine villages to the brink of starvation by the time of
the Black Death. Towards the end of the fourteenth century, peasants who had
become *mezzadri* were registered as possessing no taxable property (unless they
also owned separate plots) and thereby were protected from fiscal burdens
imposed by the city. At the same time, however, they suffered losses in
individual freedoms. Unlike their parents and grandparents, who owned their
plots, increasingly, large numbers of *mezzadri* were subjected to rules set by
landlords on short-term contracts of two years or less to blunt any attachment to
the lands they cultivated (Pinto & Pirillo; Muzzi & Nenci; and Piccini, 1987–
92). In addition, new clauses entered these labour contracts, obliging *mezzadri*
twice yearly to walk into Florence and present honorific gifts to their absentee
landlords as signs of respect and subservience, reminiscent of ancient feudal
customs (ibid.; Cohn, 1999: 19; and Herlihy, 1978, 152–3).[66]

This paradoxical relationship between economic improvement and losses of
liberties had not, however, occurred everywhere throughout Florentine
Tuscany, much less across the Italian peninsula. Peasants and herders in
Florence's upper Mugello and the Alpi fiorentine along the borders of the
Bolognese state and Romagna remained staunchly independent, but their well-
being in the post-plague Trecento followed a different path. Hit by the combined
forces of plague, war, and now crippling taxation from Florence to fend off
threats from Milanese expansion, the wealth of these mountain peasants
declined sharply from the Black Death to the end of the century, reaching its

---

[65] For Friuli, see Muir, 1993.

[66] On the favourable economics of the *mezzadria* system *c.*1375 to 1450, see section 'Equality and
Inequality: The Importance of Qualitative Evidence'.

nadir with the *estimo* of 1401. (See Figures 1–3) The following year, aided by Bolognese and Milanese armies in pursuit of conquering Florence, these peasants revolted. Unlike the much more studied urban insurrections a generation earlier – Florence's Tumulto dei Ciompi – the mountaineers were successful and cut 'handsome deals' with the Florentine state. These included fiscal exemptions for as long as fifteen years, the right to carry weapons, and new positions within the Florentine territorial state to defend Florence's borders against further incursions from enemy troops. Elected officials in mountain communes and parishes even won unique rights to decide who could settle in their communities and receive tax exemptions from Florence (Cohn, 1999: ch. 9).

Tax records are our best guides to the consequences of these successes. From the earliest *estimi* after the Black Death (1356) to the year of their revolt in 1402, Florence's northern mountaineers had become the most hammered of Florentine peasants, paying as much as thirty-five times more in taxes than those close to Florence's city walls (the commune of Mangona versus Santa Lucia Ognissanti fuori le mura; ibid. 78). But by 1402, the levers began to switch in the opposite direction, and accelerated after 1412. Propertied peasants in the mountains went from being the most impoverished villagers north of Florence to becoming the wealthiest by 1460, and, when the propertyless are considered, this increase continued until Florence's last *catasto* in 1487. Here, in contrast to the plains, there was no paradox. Political and fiscal power went hand-in-hand with climbing economic prosperity, even if the prosperity did not begin immediately with the demographic crash of 1348. Moreover, these charts illustrate no 'Malthusian traps'. From 1356 for peasants in the plains, and from 1402 for those in the mountains, propertied wealth increased – in the case of the mountaineers, by seven-fold in less than sixty years. However, these communities did not respond in Malthusian fashion. Rather, as their wealth soared, their populations remained stable or declined. Like England's later demographic response during the sixteenth to eighteenth centuries, the rising prosperity of Florence's peasantry in the Quattrocento depended on population controls – out-migration, often of women to the cities, and, given the sex-ratios of children, possibly infanticide (Cohn, 1996b: ch. 7 and chart 2.2).[67] Whether Florence's story of rising peasant wealth with population stabilization or decline characterized other Italian regions in the fifteenth century will require new economic and demographic research.

---

[67] This data concerns Florence's most populous quarter of its *contado*, Santa Maria Novella, which included the *contado*'s largest town, Prato, and had the highest concentration of large villages (more than 500 inhabitants); Herlihy and Klapisch, 1978: 236 and 238.

Political Inequality in Cities

What was the fate of Italy's urban non-elites? Like the *mezzadri*, did they experience losses in personal and political status as their wealth increased? Or, like mountain men, did their material well-being and political power progress along parallel tracks? While numerous towns and cities in northern Italy presently benefit from studies of inequality, the map of changes in the political status of non-elites has been less well populated. Florence remains the best studied. As seen in the previous section, the precise timing of lower costs of food for urban populations in Italian cities with increased production and productivity of vineyards, olive groves, and animal husbandry that improved conditions of rural and urban workers alike is difficult to determine. However, these changed conditions had certainly arrived in the city of Florence by the time of the Catasto of 1427, and in various places and for various occupations a generation or more before. Moreover, from the late fourteenth to the sixteenth centuries, with shifts in markets and the structure of textile production with increased silk production and, later, high-quality woollens (Goldthwaite, 2009), Florentine artisans benefited further, despite slumps in wool production from 1365 to the 1420s (Franceschi, 1993; 2013).[68] Similarly, silk production blossomed in other Italian cities during the fifteenth century – such as Bologna (Robertson, 2002: 51, 92), Genoa, Milan, and Venice (Tognetti, 2005) – although the industry's take-off in Venice occurred earlier in the fourteenth century (Molà, 1994).

Improved economic conditions did not, however, spawn parallel developments for artisans, shopkeepers, or other non-elites within the socio-political realm. Instead, urban elites tightened their control, curtailing earlier powers artisans had won as members of large legislative assemblies, such as the Councils of the *popolo* and *comune* in Florence, or even larger ones, as with Perugia's Council of Five Hundred, Bologna's Six Hundred, Milan's Nine Hundred, and Parma's Two Thousand. This transition in Florence's political history has been the easiest to track, in part because of the revolt of the Ciompi, with woolworkers in the vanguard, who were partially defeated in early September 1378 and more definitively in January 1382 with the overthrow of the government of lower guildsmen (*Arti Minori*). With their defeat, citizenship, guild privileges, and positions in representative assembles ended, and not only for workers in Florence's largest sector of employment (textiles); the rights and prerogatives of other non-elites – shopkeepers of various goods, bakers, butchers, cobblers, and other minor guildsmen, and even some among major-guild shopkeepers – began to lose governmental offices and power (Najemy, 2000: 82–4). With the factional conflict between

---

[68] For a general trend of greater skills fetching higher wages in textiles, see Goldthwaite, 2009: 37–40.

the Alberti and the Albizzi in the 1390s, minor guildsmen suffered further setbacks within the republic: new councils, such as that of the Two Hundred and later the Eighty, staffed by Florence's wealthiest patricians, gained control over military and other important decisions (Fubini, 1994).

By the early fifteenth century, a new bureaucratic elite, trained in law, effectively supplanted the old structure of amateur government with guildsmen serving short-term offices (Molho, 1968a; and Molho, 1968b). According to John Najemy, 'By 1400 the *popolo* had acquiesced in the elite's leadership and emerging dominance. After this point, organized challenges from the guild community no longer materialized' (Najemy, 1991: 280; and Najemy, 2006b: 182–7). Moreover, between 1403 and the exile of the Medici in 1433, the possibilities for new families to acquire political offices declined, even if positions for minor guildsmen initially increased in the city's pool of candidates for political offices (Fubini, 1991: 227; and Najemy, 2006b: 184–5). With the return and triumph of the Medici in 1434, guild rights deteriorated further, with power concentrating in the hands of merchant elites through networks of patronage (D.V. Kent, 1978; and Padgett, 1993). Legal and illegal forms of intimidation, systematic use of exile, and hired thugs to execute 'justice' in back alleyways became increasingly common (Martines, 2005: 31–4).[69] With Cosimo's grandson, Lorenzo il Magnifico, republicanism disappeared in all but name, especially after the failed Pazzi conspiracy of 1478, achieved by constitutional measures, such as the creation of a Council of Seventy, and ruthless revenge against his enemies Now, members of ancient elite Florentine families joined artisans and shopkeepers in being frozen out of power, unless they could enter Laurentian patronage networks (Brown, 1994; F.W. Kent, 1994: 53–5; Mallett, 1989: v–xii).

Steadily through the fifteenth century, citizens' abilities to bargain and petition for collective privileges, such as rights to bear arms, election to local offices, grants of tax concessions, and governmental assistance for damages of war, fire, plague, and other natural disasters, had almost entirely disappeared.[70] In their place, as attested by thousands of letters now preserved in the Medici archives that mounted exponentially through the second half of the fifteenth century, individuals could beseech Medici lords to grant concessions for tax relief, remissions of criminal charges, or awards of minor posts in the provinces in exchange for obedience and loyalty (Brucker, 1983; Connell, 2000, ch. 3; D.V. Kent, 2000; F.W. Kent, 1987b; F.W. Kent, 2002; and F.W.

---

[69] For Lorenzo's reliance on thugs, see references for 'potenze', below; for his use of 'staffieri' in the countryside following the Pazzi conspiracy, see F.W. Kent, 2005: 400.

[70] On these collective petitions, see Cohn, 1999, part III; by the 1450s they declined sharply within the acts of the *Provvisioni* (Archivio di Stato, Firenze) and, after 1478, they disappear. F.W.

Kent, 2005). Nevertheless, at least one new collectivity of the poor emerged. Youth gangs known as *potenze* patrolled neighbourhoods. In return for Lorenzo's patronage, they heeded his calls in times of need, such as after the Pazzi conspiracy when 'the boys of the Millstone Corner, numbering thirty or more', assassinated the Medici's enemies (F.W. Kent, 2005: 391; F.W. Kent, 1987a; Rosenthal, 2006; and Trexler, 1980). These informal powers rendered through new patronage networks were, however, a far cry from the previous corporative and constitutional rights non-elite guildsmen enjoyed from the late thirteenth to the early fifteenth centuries. By the end of Cosimo's rule, artisan power had transmogrified into a new atomized 'Renaissance individualism'. Now artisans, shopkeepers, and even merchants had become dependent on Medicean noblesse oblige.

Italy's other republics followed similar trajectories: by 1390 Lucca's Guinigi family implemented what Cosimo de' Medici was unable to achieve until a half-century later: dynastic rule bearing a republican scaffolding, with artisan representation as mostly a formality (Meek, 1978). Other city-states, such as Bologna, where broad artisan representation had been largely lost by Cardinal Albornoz's expansion of the papal states in the 1350s, marked similar late-fourteenth- and fifteenth-century pathways. After a successful revolt in 1376 that brought papal power temporarily to an end in Bologna, artisans regained their representation in broad city councils. Their gains were, however, short-lived. In 1393 the city's leading families seriously limited the powers of guildsmen, replacing the Council of Six Hundred with an emergency Council of the Sixteen. By the middle of the fifteenth century, it became a permanent body through which a tightly knit group of between twenty and twenty-five oligarchic families converted communal guild government into 'the Bentivolesco financial-political oligarchy' (to use Ian Robertson's expression). Under the leadership of the Bentivoglio, these families in effect possessed hereditary control over the state and pilfered its resources as though they were private patrimonies. A generation before Florence's Pazzi conspiracy, this collegiate oligarchy possessed the financial and governmental powers that Lorenzo il Magnifico achieved only after draconian reforms in 1480 (Ady, 1937; and Robertson, 2002).[71]

Venice may appear as an exception in that its closing of ranks to include political elites alone came a half-century before the Black Death: 'the Serrata of the Great Council' in 1297. Venetian historians, however, have shown that the

---

[71] On Lorenzo de' Medici's financial corruption and increased authority in the last decades of his rule, see Brown, 1994. Unlike his previous work on Cesena (Robertson, 1985), Robertson, 2002, pays less attention to the consequences for artisan representation in Bologna after Paul II's tighter control and management of the papal states in the 1460s.

tightening of security, strengthening of the Council of Ten, and further closing of the nobility's ranks progressed through the fifteenth and sixteenth centuries (Judde de Larivière & Salzberg, 2013; and Romano, 2020). Stanley Chojnacki has emphasized a subsequent moment in the Venetian aristocracy's concentration of power: 'The Second Serrata', in the early fifteenth century (Chojnacki, 1994).

Of course, north of the Apennines rule by the *popolo* (artisans, shopkeepers, and often merchants) and republican councils had less lengthy histories. Philip Jones dismissed republicanism there as 'an episode between two periods of aristocratic rule' (Jones, 1997: 585; and Scott, 2012, ch. 3).[72] By 1250 the *popolo* had fallen to signorial dynasties at Milan (the Visconti), Padua (the della Scala), Mantua (the Gonzaga), Ferrara (the Este), and Urbino (the Montefeltro), as well as in numerous smaller city-states, where dynasties rotated in rapid succession.[73] Yet the historiography of these political events has often followed too closely the class bias of contemporary chroniclers. Historians have concentrated on political and social relations at the top of these societies: battles between patrician factions and the hegemony of single ruling families. Few have investigated the rights and prerogatives of citizens more broadly under these so-called 'despots' or in aristocratic republics such as Venice (Judde de Larivière and Salzberg, 2013; and Judde de Larivière & Van Gelder, 2020).[74] The role of guilds and the existence of broad councils – such as Parma's Two Thousand, which survived through the fourteenth century even under the rule of a Neapolitan king (Cohn, 2006: 140 and 290), and Bologna's Six Hundred, which lasted to the end of the fifteenth century under oligarchic control of families loyal to the Bentivoglio and by 1460 under the thumb of the papacy – need further study (Robertson, 2002, 49–63). Moreover, even when these broad representative bodies largely comprised of artisans, shopkeepers, and members of guilds had been banished, popular memories of them could endure as seen with the revival of the Council of Five Hundred in Perugia. After a revolt of the *popolo* against the papacy and Perugia's aristocracy in 1535, not only was this council restored, but citizens soon expanded their constituency with a new Council of Six Hundred.[75] Similar revivals and expansions of representation and offices for non-elites occurred in other cities, such as Milan in 1515, Brescia in 1517, and Lucca in 1531.[76]

---

[72] On the false distinctions between republican and 'despotic' governments, see Fantoni, 2020.

[73] For cities such as Perugia, Bologna, Padua, Asti, Pisa, and Bergamo, see Scott, 2012, ch. 3, where rule by the *popolo* survived intermittently into the fifteenth century.

[74] See also Mackenney, 1987: ch. 5: 'for the first time, merchants began to insist on their separateness and superiority, and sought to claw their way to legal privileges above craftsmen and boatmen' (223).

[75] *La Cronica perugina cinquecentesca*, 209–10; and Cohn, 2021.

[76] For these and many further examples from 1494 to 1559, see Cohn, 2021.

Where historians have peered beneath politics at the top into the world of day-to-day decision-making at the neighbourhood level, as Ian Robertson has done for Cesena, 1378 to 1465, artisans are seen holding neighbourhood elections and serving minor offices as tax collectors, despite their cities no longer possessing broad legislative assemblies (Robertson, 1987). The same has been recently explored with the soft power of the *popolo* in Venice, who possessed no formal legislative powers (Judde de Larivière & Van Gelder, 2020). Even beneath the signorial rule of the powerful Visconti dukes of Milan, the institutions of the city's ancient commune continued to survive, including its broad-base Council of Nine Hundred, comprised of merchants and the upper echelons of the artisan and guild community. According to Francesco Cognasso, Milan's government was a combination of signorial and communal institutions – a diarchy – and in times of crises, as in 1402–3, 1412, and 1447, the duchess or duke had to negotiate new reforms by assembling the old communal councils (Cognasso, 1955a: 77, 90–3, 157–9; and Cognasso, 1955b, 396–7, and 399–403).

More recently, Paolo Grillo has emphasized 'the longa durata' of popular institutions, such as the territorial officers of the neighbourhoods (*vicinie*), the gate districts, the 'elders' of the parishes, and especially that of the *Capitano del Popolo*. These 'republican' institutions limited the powers of the Milanese dukes, supported popular resistance in periods of crisis, and maintained a collective memory of popular powers at least until the mid-fifteenth century (Grillo, 2012). Even into the sixteenth century, market towns in the duchy – such as Caravaggio, Agnadello, Pagazzano, Vailate, and others – maintained their local power structures of the *vicinitas*, where collectively citizens enjoyed a degree of power and heads of households (*capifamiglie*) performed crucial tasks such as the distribution of local taxes. In some places, heads of families continued to assemble periodically under the porticoes of their communal palaces to elect local representatives, who drafted petitions to the central government or could form general assemblies (Di Tullio, 2011: ch. 2). Under the papal monarchy of late medieval and Renaissance Rome, artisans still elected their officials of neighbourhood districts (*rioni*), and these were more than honorific positions. Through the first half of the fifteenth century, revolts of the Roman *popolo*, led by elected neighbour captains and under neighbourhood banners, struggled against tax policies and dictates imposed by the curia: they continued to banish popes and their entourage of officers and courtiers from the Eternal City (Cohn, 2006). How these rights and responsibilities of a broad base of citizens, along with the constitutional powers of great assemblies and representation, may have changed from the Black Death to the sixteenth century remain uncharted waters.

Nonetheless, as with the republics, the direction of change is one of decline in artisan rights in these northern city- and territorial states, despite moments of popular resurgence, as at Milan in 1403 following the death of Giangaleazzo Visconti (Grillo, 2012: 227–30). In Cesena, for example, the Malatesta's loss of power to the papacy in 1465 also swept artisans from their rule at the parish level (Robertson, 1987). In the Milanese territory of the Geradadda, Matteo Di Tullio has recently shown that only two communities continued to possess late medieval general assemblies of citizens by the sixteenth century; and, in other market towns, local governing bodies had transformed into narrow oligarchies of elites. In Caravaggio, for instance, 95 per cent of its families produced less than 3 per cent of elected representatives ('consiglieri') by the sixteenth century (Di Tullio, 2011: 70).

Northern Italy in a Broader European Context

Cities in other regions of Europe followed roughly parallel political pathways across the same economic terrain of non-elite prosperity and narrowing economic inequality. In late-fourteenth- and fifteenth-century London, artisans lost their authority to control quality standards of their own production, rights to elect aldermen and mayors, and rights to serve in minor municipal posts (Barron, 2004; and Williams, 1963). These losses became deeply apparent with John of Northampton's mayoral defeat and banishment in 1384. Even after the suppression of his rivals and execution of his principal adversary and the mayor after him, Nicholas Brembre, during the Merciless Parliament of 1386, there was no turning back to pre-plague artisan representation and freedoms. Instead, with royal intervention, the century's end spelled the opposite: further concentration of political power within the hands of London magnates. From 1387 onwards, rights of citizenship narrowed: those born to fathers who were freemen were no longer guaranteed citizenship. Now they were required to prove it by registering with the city chamberlain and be sworn in as freemen (Tucker, 2007: 23). In the 1440s London's ruling elites smashed craftsmen's last attempts to have their earlier electoral rights recognized (Barron, 1990; Barron, 2004; Rigby, 1998, 69).

For craftsmen and other burgesses of English monastic boroughs, the decline in liberties was more devastating than for Londoners. After the defeat and severe reprisals for rebels at Bury St Edmunds and St Albans in the summer of 1381, not only were their short-lived charters destroyed, concessions gained earlier in the fourteenth century were rolled back (Faith, 1981; Freeman, 2008: 96–8; Lobel, 1935; Trenholme, 1927). Until the dissolution of the monasteries, artisans, and even merchants, as in St Albans, were not recognized as citizens but were legally designated as 'villeins' subject to monastic lords. The burgesses' defeat at Bury St Edmunds in 1381 was so crushing that later protest, even through legitimate channels such as lawsuits and petitions, all but disappeared. Major national conflicts, such as Cade's Rebellion in 1450 and the Wars of Roses, failed to rekindle earlier dreams of political liberties. Even Henry VIII's dissolution of the monasteries from 1536 failed to re-awaken these burgesses' earlier civic ambitions (Lobel, 1935, 163 and 167).

Another scenario of post-plague or post-1381 English cities suggests some success with new charters of incorporation, first in Bristol in 1373, with at least six more following for other principal cities during the first half of the fifteenth century (Weinbaum, 1937: 63–96). But as Christian Liddy has shown, these were rights that consolidated the power of these cities' ruling elites in national politics in partnership with the crown (Liddy, 2005: 228). As a consequence, not only did the balance of power shift towards narrower oligarchic rule, it also enabled elites to impose a greater, disproportionate share of the royal tax burden onto the poor, at least in cities (Dyer, 1995: 188–9).[77]

As for Flanders, with Philip van Artevelde's defeat at Rozebeke in 1382, craft representation in municipal governments in Flemish cities declined, and especially at Bruges after its unsuccessful revolts in 1437–8. Craftsmen lost all rights to elect representatives to city councils. The duke of Burgundy, and elite merchants who did his bidding, now controlled these formerly 'representative' bodies. At Bruges, another rebellion proved successful in 1477, allowing craftsmen in coalition with merchants to return to power. It lasted only a generation, however (Dumolyn & Haemers, 2005; Haemers, 2005; Haemers, 2009).

A similar revival of non-elite political power is seen in some Castilian towns. Armed revolt, moreover, was not the only route by which artisans could revive their former corporatist political power. As in many English and northern Italian towns, artisans in Castilian cities had lost their corporative privileges and rights of election during the last quarter of the fourteenth century. However, between 1475 and 1511 guildsmen in towns along the northern coast of the Iberian Peninsula successfully protested against the powers of an entrenched nobility. As Jesús Angel Solórzano Telechea has shown, these ends were achieved through oath-taking and assemblies without armed resistance. The artisans took their protest to the king of Castile, demanded electoral reforms, and accused their noble rulers of abuses of justice, unfair taxation, and usurpation of artisans' former rights to electoral offices. With the Ordinances of Vitoria in 1476, which spread to seventeen other coastal towns, guild communities allied with the king against the old

---

[77] Based on testamentary evidence, Dyer, 2012, may have changed his mind; however, his conclusions on elite support of poor neighbours also rested here with villages and small towns.

lineages. In some towns, guildsmen even banned the nobility from holding office. The alliance between the crown and these 'middling sorts',[78] however, rapidly reinstated a new oligarchy in these towns composed of the upper echelons of the guild community, such as at Chincilla in 1484. Moreover, such alliances between the crown and non-elites were not the rule. For the rest of Castile, craftsmen's strategies to regain their late-fourteenth-century prerogatives were different. They protested not only against patricians but also against the king, expelling royal magistrates and proclaiming their towns to be independent city-states. In the second decade of the sixteenth century, they formed a Holy League against the crown, but were defeated in 1521 and lost any further opportunities to revive their former fourteenth-century guild representation (Solórzano Telechea, 2014).

Finally, not all European cities easily fit what I now hypothesize as the general paradox of a sharp decline in artisans' political power and status, when post-plague economics began enriching peasants, artisans, and shop-keepers, thereby threatening the social distinctions of merchant and noble oligarchies. One example is Lisbon. Because of artisan support in 1383 for the regency of the Master of Avis, the crown granted guildsmen powers to maintain law and order and a voice in municipal affairs by establishing the electoral body of the Twenty-Four (Yerushalmi, 1976: 28). This institution endured until the massacre of 'New Christians' (recently converted Jews) in April 1506, staged mainly by the lower echelons of Lisbon's citizens. To punish them and extend his regal powers, King Manuel abolished the Council of Twenty-Four, replacing Lisbon's municipal government with his own personal rule.[79] Another brief interlude of political equality occurred in Cologne after the revolt of the Neubürger against the city's old patrician families in 1396. From its success, some artisans gained limited rights and a say in city government. These rights, however, lasted only into the first decade of the fifteenth century, when Cologne's patricians restored their monopoly powers (Militzer, 1980, 102–9).

To test the paradoxical relation between strides in economic well-being and equality on the one hand and political decline and inequality on the other, further towns in Western and Eastern Europe, along with regions south of Rome, require large-collaborative, pan-European research compar-able to Alfani's on inequality. But for now, especially for northern and central Italy, despite variations in post-plague economic equalities and political inequalities, I hypothesize that the paradoxical patterns between non-elites' economic prosperity and their decline in political powers and

---

[78] On notions of 'middling sorts' in early modern English history, see Smith, 2017: 39.

[79] On the massacre and end of guild power in Lisbon, see Damião de Gois, *Chronica do felicissimo rey dom Emanuel*; Cohn, 2018: 130–1; and Yerushalmi, 1976.

status sketched earlier will hold. The usual assumptions that powers in the political and economic spheres invariably evolved along parallel tracks – one intrinsically supporting the other – need to be questioned, and not only for the post–Black Death century.[80] We now venture into further uncharted waters: the cultural life of non-elites within the contexts of post–Black Death equality and inequality.

3 Cultural Inequality

Growth of Cultural Divisions Within the Labouring Classes

The previous section highlighted the paradoxical decline in artisans' and shop-keepers' political power against the backdrop of their growing prosperity and economic equality. This political decline remains best studied for Florence, and its discussion hinges on the defeat of a broad-based coalition of disenfranchised woolworkers and minor guildsmen from mid-July 1378 to the defeat of the government of the *Arti Minori* in January 1382. As John Najemy has vigorously argued, these defeats initiated the long decline of Florentine guilds as economic and political forces in Florentine society. In his words, the *popolo* 'became docile clients of elite patrons' (Najemy, 2006a: 41). Yet artisans and shop-keepers in other Italian city-states without revolts of Ciompi experienced similar downward political trajectories over much the same period, seen not only in constitutional losses but also by social quiescence, as suggested by a steep decline in the numbers of popular revolts and protests reported in chronicles until the Italian Wars in 1494 (Cohn, 2021).

For Florence, loss of collective power and representation for artisans had not resulted solely from constitutional changes. As scholars of fifteenth-century art and political patronage have shown, loyal subjects, even ones down the social ladder, could succeed within the new structures of favours, letters of recom-mendation, and patronage circles ('*amicizia*') that extended from the Medici and other well-placed families. This patronage system had a double effect on the guild community: first, it atomized power, diluting and fragmenting older corporatist ideals and possibilities of collective action. Second, it widened divisions within the lower classes of minor guildsmen and disenfranchised workers, creating a more clearly defined 'middling sort' in Florentine urban society (Najemy, 2006b, 182–6, 266). Certain ambitious and skilled labourers in textiles or other trades could now engineer political and economic advantages for their families in alliance with and out of loyalty to patrician patrons, rather

---

[80] For recent assumptions that these connections were mutually supportive over the long term, see Piketty, 2020.

than in solidarity with less skilled workers, the *popolo minuto*, as had happened in 1378.

This growing division between 'respectable' artisans and those beneath them finds corroboration in the post-plague history of charity. In Florence and other cities of northern and central Italy, a dramatic change occurred in individuals' choices of charity to address poverty during the last quarter of the fourteenth century.[81] From pious bequests made indiscriminately to the 'poor of Christ', testators turned to dowry funds to support selected young girls, chosen according to their own and their families' *buon costume* (Cohn, 1992: 65–7; Henderson, 1988). As Wim Blockmans and Jelle Haemers have shown for the Low Countries (Blockmans, 1980; Haemers, 2009), and others for England (Hindle, 2000: 115, 227; Walter, 2006, 49–58; Wood, 2008, ch. 5; Wrightson, 1982), such a reshaping of class lines within the working and artisan classes was not peculiar to Florentine history. Changes in poor relief, the upsurge of guides to good manners, and attention to elocution and language formed new and more distinctive divisions within communities beneath the merchant classes. As Frank Rexroth has shown for London, these divisions – greater rewards for the upper echelons of loyal and productive artisans and labourers, and greater vilification and persecution of new immigrants, the truly poor, and other outcasts – were two sides of the same coin. These divisions did not need to wait until the sixteenth century, as early modernists have often assumed.[82] Instead, at least in London, they became the conscious objectives of elite politics in the wake of the Uprising of 1381 (Rexroth, 2007, ch. 6) – that is, at almost exactly the same time that similar class divisions were forming in the city of Florence (Najemy, 2006b: 182–6, 266).[83] The emergence of a middling sort, with sharper divisions between rich and poor within communities of labourers, has until now been studied within regional boundaries as though they were sui generis developments and not ones then sweeping across wide swaths of Western Europe. I hypothesize that these developments relate to the threats of rising equality and new patron–client relations that also cut across city-state and national boundaries and were embedded in the larger demographics of the Black Death.

Satire

Rising equality and new ties of patronage that profited the middling sorts, while subordinating them to ruling elites, paralleled the countervailing political

---

[81] For a parallel case drawn from English testaments, see Dyer, 2012.

[82] See Smith, 2017, for English historians beyond those cited above, and that 'the principal employers of labour [were] fashion[ing] a more deferential labour force' in the fifteenth century.

[83] More work is needed on manners and customs from the Black Death to the fifteenth century across Europe.

developments seen in the previous section. Given the new and sudden demographic realities and their eventual effects on labour markets, evidence from a variety of sources points to elites driving a distinctive wedge between themselves and those beneath them, who had been the principal beneficiaries of the Black Death's demographic silver lining. New literary works satirizing non-elites take off after the Black Death, as with Boccaccio's *Decameron*, but much more so from the late fourteenth century through the Renaissance in stories (*novelle*) by Franco Sacchetti, Giovanni Sercambi, Gentile Sermini, Giovanni Pontano, and Angelo Firenzuola, and the still shorter stories (*facezie*) of the mid-fifteenth-century humanist Poggio Bracciolini, Angelo Poliziano, the Piovano Arlotto, and others.[84] For the most part, these belittled peasants from the countryside, some for their poverty and absence of civilization (literally, their ignorance of the ways of the city) as Sermini expressed it at the end of one of his stories: it would have been better to have died in the plague of 1424 in civilized Siena 'than to have died a thousand times a day' with the beasts of the mountains [his hosts], who had never seen a city'.[85] As this literature progressed from Boccaccio into the fifteenth century, it became more aggressive, moralistic, and mean-spirited (Bec, 1981: 40). After all, various stories in the *Decameron* ended in praise of peasants, giving them the last laugh, as with the stately and patient peasant wife of the Marquis of Saluzzo (Day 10, story 10) or the deaf mute of Lamporecchio (Day 3, story 1). Non-elites could even win the moral high ground over nobles, as achieved by the Florentine baker Cisti through his wit, foresight, and noble character in his dealings with the nobleman Messer Geri Spina (Day 6, story 2).

By the fifteenth century, the tone of these stories had changed. Just after the plague of 1424, Sermini drafted a short ethnography of mountain peasants south of Siena. He described their rustic and crude vocabulary – 'i loro grossi e rustici vocabolacci' – and scripted a 'sonetta' of their supposed animal utterances to reproach their speech. He details their clothing, down to their wearing the same dirty and oily underwear day in and out; their stinking diet of garlic, leeks, and radishes; their hairstyle, 'cut with shears used for castrating their sheep', which left them 'resembling the billy goats they bred'; their hovels, 'filled with the fumes of their animals and the stench of human excrement'; and their incomprehension of church services, howling with their hands shoved down their throats. Each of these topics ended with the same refrain: 'little separated these men from the beasts they bred'.[86]

---

[84] *Facezie e motti*.

[85] *Le novella di Gentile Sermini*: Novella XII: 'L'autore e ser Cecco da Perugia', 169–81; citation on 181.

[86] *Le novella di Gentile Sermini*; and Cohn, 2009: 110–12.

The new literature also attacked non-elites in cities, and especially those seen to have overstepped their social station. In another story, Sermini mocked a recent immigrant to Siena, rumoured to have been elected to the city's governing council. As a result, citizens kidnapped him, dressed him up as king of the carnival, and humiliated him, all to great applause from the storyteller.[87] The poet, storyteller, and Florentine statesmen Franco Sacchetti, in one of his *Trecentonovelle*, written towards the end of the fourteenth century, mocked a fat artisan ('grossolano artefice'), who was also a shopkeeper ('*uomo di picciolo affare*') but whose Christian name is never given.[88] Sacchetti scorned the parvenu's arrogance for having imagined that he might invent a family coat of arms for himself, as though 'belonging to the French royal family'. More galling, the artisan approached Giotto ('the greatest painter of his time') to invent and paint these arms on a shield the artisan brought to Giotto's shop. To humiliate the upstart, Giotto handed the commission to his apprentice, with instructions to smear the shield with every military cliché imaginable: 'a helmet, a neck guard, a pair of armlets, a pair of iron gloves, front and back cuirasses, upper thigh and leg guards, a sword, knife, a lance'. When the patron returned for his finished goods, he exploded, shouting he'd not pay four pennies for the mess, providing Giotto further opportunities to humiliate the fat-so 'for lacking any trace of antiquity'. The artisan called the police, who, of course, sided with the great Giotto, rubbing salt into the artisan's wounds.[89] Such stories of ridicule continue into the fifteenth century, such as that of a rich barber named Licinus who built a monumental tomb for himself which, because of his low status, gained ridicule for his presumptuousness from his elite neighbours.[90]

Certainly, this literature calls for more study, especially beyond the borders of Tuscany. As with fiscal records and Gini coefficients before the Black Death, little evidence of these works survives before 1348 to compare with the early Renaissance. Nonetheless, attitudes and nuances from this literature can be plotted across the following century and a half as elite authors sharpened their barbs against peasants, artisans, and shopkeepers. Finally, historians, at least of late medieval England, have interpreted sumptuary legislation as another field of elite assault on servants, labourers, and artisans, who used their post-plague economic advantage to improve their lives, and, in so doing, threatened social distinctions (Dyer, 1984: 23; Dyer, 2000: 27, 35; Du Boulay, 1970: 11; Hatcher, 1998: 79; Prestwich, 1980: 142). These historians have focused on one set of

---

[87] *Le novelle di Gentile Sermini*, Novella XXX, also, Bec, 1981: 44.
[88] Bec, 1981, observes that these stories stripped peasants of 'all their identity and individuality' (42).
[89] Franco Sacchetti, *Il Trecentonovelle*, Novella LXIII, 122–3.
[90] Nelson and Zeckhauser, 2008: 56, for this and other stories in fifteenth-century Florence.

sumptuary restrictions: the national statutes of the realm for 1363 that punished those beneath 'merchants, citizens, burgesses, manufacturers, and craft masters' for expenditures on a wide range of luxury foods, clothing, and ornaments.[91]

By contrast, for Italy from 1200 to 1500, 300 statute books or statutes found scattered within more general compilations restricted expenditures on banquets, weddings, funerals, dowries, clothes, ornaments, and diet. Yet here historians have not pointed to elites at any time promulgating these laws principally to impede peasants or artisans from rising above their station. Diane Hughes has even argued the opposite: the *popolo* used sumptuary legislation to 'fetter the aristocrat' (Hughes, 2002).[92] Furthermore, historians of Italy have yet to consider whether the Black Death or later plagues were at all pivotal for increases in this legislation. However, for Florence (which possesses the greatest number of these laws), the annual numbers increase sharply after the Black Death and concentrate during the next century and a quarter, especially from 1348 to 1400.[93] Moreover, 'the most comprehensive compilation' of Florentine sumptuary laws 'to date' was enacted in 1356, and it served as the template for further sumptuary legislation for the remainder of the century (Rainey, 1985, 146). However, by Ronald Rainey's synopsis of its forty-three chapters, the principal targets of the restrictions were women, with few exemptions by social class and without mentioning any artisan professions (Rainey, 1985, ch. 3). Nonetheless, more attention should be given to these laws beyond England as mechanisms of elite distinction.

We now turn to another source that can be quantified with greater numbers and precision: artistic commissions found in last wills and testaments. These stretch across much of the Italian peninsula and tap directly into trends in cultural inequality after the Black Death. I here introduce a pilot study based on five towns in Tuscany and Umbria, which does not focus on Florence alone.

Artistic Commissions

The commissions embedded in last wills were almost without exception for works to be displayed in ecclesiastical institutions: parish churches, friaries, nunneries, monasteries, and hospitals.[94] Beyond aesthetics, they highlight subjects in religious history, notions of family, and ideologies of the self. What is especially surprising is the number of them that derive from non-elites:

---

[91] 'Sumptuary Legislation, 1363', in Horrox, 1994: 341.

[92] See Killerby, 2002: 80, who contests Hughes' assertion.

[93] Based on ibid., table 2.1, 28–30. Florence possesses 61; Venice comes second with 42. Before 1348, 13 sumptuary statutes survive in Florence, or 0.09 per annum; for 1348 to 1399, 22 (0.42 per annum); for 1400 to 1475, 23 (0.30 per annum); and for 1476–1500, 3 (0.12); my calculations.

[94] For my operational definition of this 'art' found in testamentary commissions, see below.

shopkeepers, artisans, peasants, and even a disenfranchised woolworker.[95] Yet art historians have rarely touched this body of material. The reasons may be obvious. Few of them can presently be connected to surviving works of art found in churches, museums, or private collections.[96] As I will argue, the widespread disappearance of these objects did not rest only or predominantly on the vagaries of time, weather, fires, and wars.

Another reason why art historians have ignored these commissions concerns an essential difference between them and ones found in notarial contracts. While the latter were agreements between patrons and artists, testamentary commissions almost never mentioned artists. Instead, they described – sometimes in great detail – the desired compositions, specifying the number and names of the testator's chosen saints, where they should appear in the composition, and often the amount their executors should pay. In testamentary commissions of the late Middle Ages and early Renaissance, I have thus far found only one artist named in these contracts. The 1312 will of the Florentine 'Discretus vir' Ricchuccius filius quondam [hereafter, f.q.] Puccii from the parish of Santa Maria Novella mentions Giotto twice, but in neither case was Giotto the artist the testator wished to execute a testamentary commission. Instead, Giotto is mentioned as the painter of an altarpiece, where the testator wished to supply oil annually to illuminate the painting in Santa Maria Novella. His second mention relates to a painting he commissioned earlier: 'a beautiful panel' painted by 'the exalted Giotto' in the Dominican friary at Prato.[97]

Evidence of artistic commissions from peasants or artisans derive almost exclusively from one source: last wills and testaments. These are scattered throughout thousands of notarial books or appear in parchments preserved by ecclesiastic institutions.[98] Few of these were repeated in separate notarial contracts, yet the testamentary commissions were not wish-lists. Rather, as Michele Bacci has shown, they were legally binding contracts and, if not executed, could end in civil lawsuits.[99] Such works of art from non-elites were commissioned

---

[95] For my operational definition of 'non-elites' as seen in these testaments, see below.

[96] For several of these survivals, see Bacci, 2000: 372, as with Bartolo di Fredi's triptych with Mary and Saints John the Baptist and John Evangelist, from *c.* 1380, in the Museum of Lucignano. The triptych bears witness to Ser Griffo's testamentary commission in 1365. For several others in Trecento Pisa, see Cannon, 2013: 257–9. Also, for a later period, see Plazzotta, et al. 2006: 72, for an altarpiece painted by Perugino in a chapel of Santa Maria dei Servi, Perugia, commissioned by the carpenter Giovanni Schiavone in his will of 7 April 1507.

[97] ASF, *Diplomatico* [hereafter, ASF], *Diplomatico* [hereafter, *Dipl.*], Santa Maria Novella, 15 June 1312.

[98] I collected this archival data in the late 1980s; for further examples, see Cohn, 1992; Cohn, 1996a; Cohn, 2012; and, most recently, Cohn, 2020.

[99] Bacci, 2000, especially chs. IV: 'Immagini come strumenti di salvezza: opere d'arte e lasciti testamentari', 227–328; and V: 'Dalle volontà testamentarie all'opera finita', 329–430.

principally for parish churches, friaries, or monasteries. A rare exception was a commission by a blacksmith from the Mugello, north of Florence: on his deathbed, he left 14 *lire* to adorn his bed with an image 'in the likeness of the majesty of God', bequeathed to the hospital of Borgo San Lorenzo to care for the poor.[100] Other commissions for painted or carved figures could cost less. For instance, a disenfranchised Florentine wool carder bequeathed a candlestick holder to the hospital of Santa Maria Nuova and ordered it to be 'painted and inscribed' with his coats of arms, even though this woolworker possessed no family name and most likely no previous coats of arms.[101] Franco Sacchetti's anxieties (described earlier) resonate beyond fiction.

To get a sense of what these prices meant for the household budgets of artisans, we return to Richard Goldthwaite's grain prices and real wages, along with figures on food consumption detailed by Lodovico Ghetti in 1445. With considerable arithmetic for consumption and costs of wheat, wine, meat, oil, Ghetti estimated it would cost a worker 12 florins a year to live a healthy life, presumably with a small family. At an exchange rate of between 4 and 5 *lire* per florin in mid-fifteenth-century Florence, this would amount to around 54 *lire*. Food accounted for the lion's share of an artisan's expenses: as high as 80 per cent of the budget, giving an annual expenditure of around 67 *lire*. Rent and clothing were relatively cheap (Goldthwaite, 1980: 346–7). However, as noted earlier, the mid-fifteenth century would have been near the apex of artisan prosperity, not only for the late Middle Ages and the Renaissance, but in southern Europe perhaps until the end of the nineteenth century.[102] As Goldthwaite estimates, 'an ordinary mason or smith on a construction site had an optimum income of 175 to 200 *lire* [per annum], and the income range extended upwards to . . . 250 to 300 *lire* for better-paid foremen'. Other salaried employees could earn more, as with Nofri di Biagio, who worked at the hospital of the *Innocenti* from 1445 to 1447, earning 350 *lire* a year (ibid., 348–9). These employees certainly would not be classified as workers. On the other hand, they were without a family name and not on the same economic plane as Florentine merchants, even ones of the local economy. Instead, they correspond to the upper reaches of the grey area I define later as respectable *popolani*, whose wealth climbed substantially during the post– Black Death century.

As discovered in Section 1, while the income and wealth of artisans and large proportions of non-elite populations continued to climb through the first half of

---

[100] ASF, *Dipl.*, S. Maria Nuova, 21 September 1323.

[101] ASF, *Dipl.*, Ospedale di Santa Maria Nuova, 24 August 1368.

[102] As seen in Section 1, Hatcher and others (Hatcher, 1998 and 2013; Hatcher & Stephenson, 2019) challenge such long-range comparisons based on real wages.

the fifteenth century, this depended not on increases in their nominal wages, which remained stubbornly stable or 'sticky', as scholars from Adam Smith to John Munro have described them.[103] Rather, wages rose because the prices of commodities declined. The buying power of artisans and other non-elites would have been much less in the late Trecento than those calculated by Ghetti in 1445. Nonetheless, his figures do not go much beyond what officials of the Florentine *catasto* calculated for expenditures on basic commodities eighteen years earlier in 1427 (Goldthwaite, 1980: 347–8). Fifteen years before that (1412), however, a week's salary for an unskilled worker was 10 *soldi*, the equivalent of around 18.5 *lire* or about 5 florins a year, calculated on an annual working year of 260 days (Brucker, 1977: 322). Given Ghetti's notion of a 'healthy life', c. 1445, such a salary would have been well below subsistence level. Yet we know that by the 1360s artisans were able to purchase luxury items and, in some cases, landed property in the nearby countryside.[104] Moreover, as seen earlier with la Roncière's and Goldthwaite's data, the wages of unskilled workers were rising faster than those of skilled artisans. If we reach back further, to 1385 and to the lower echelons of the elites, the annual salary of the physician Coluccio Bonavia was 40 florins.[105] Given that the rate of exchange between the florin and the *lire* had depreciated over this period by as much as a quarter, the physician's salary would have been approximately 140 *lire* – 40 per cent of the much less prestigious hospital employee Nofri di Biagio sixty years later and, no doubt, only a fraction of physicians' pay two generations later.[106] While annual incomes for the mid-fifteenth century certainly overstate the possibilities for artisans or other non-elites to commission works of art from 1348 to 1425, even for the unskilled worker in 1412, a ten-*lire* burial painting would constitute six months or less of income during the latter half of the fourteenth century, and thus with savings over a lifetime would have been conceivable for the frugal worker in a last gesture for personal and family remembrance. Moreover, as examples will show, such commissions could cost even less.

Ideals of Remembrance

The goals of these artisan commissions for engraved candlestick holders, embroidered figures for priestly vestments, panel and wall paintings, and wax figures that could cost less than a florin (less than 4 *lire* in the late fourteenth century) were not just for salvation. As with pious bequests from elites, those of humble testators expressed desires for remembrance and prestige in this world along with the next.

---

[103] On notions of wage stickiness back to Smith, see Caferro, 2018: 131.   [104] See Section 1.

[105] *Il Memoriale di Iacopo di Coluccino Bonavia Medico Lucchese*, 209.

[106] Park, 1985: 81; the medical profession became more lucrative in the fifteenth century than it had been in the fourteenth vis-à-vis other professions.

Furthermore, they demanded that their images be painted 'in their very likeness (*ad similitudinem*)' and occasionally specified that their images were to be flanked by selectively mentioned deceased family members. Such was a testamentary commission by a blacksmith living in the Aretine hill town Bibbiena. His modest testament centred on one bequest alone: a panel to be painted of the Virgin and Child, with St John the Evangelist on one side, and Mary Magdalene and St Anthony on the other, to be hung close to his grave in the friary of the Blessed Mary. The blacksmith's instructions then went further: on one side, the artist was to paint the blacksmith kneeling at the Virgin's feet and, on the other, his deceased father. For neighbours and future generations not to miss his point, the blacksmith commanded the future unnamed artist to label the figures: 'Here lies Montagne the blacksmith; there, Pasquino, his father.'[107] Other artisan commissions could supply more details, as with one from an Aretine green-grocer (*ortolanus*) in his will of 1371. For a mere 4 *lire*, he commissioned narratives (*ystorie*) of the Holy Ghost to be placed above the altar of his confraternity, perhaps as the *predella* of an existing painting. His testament gives further clues to his social and economic standing. His largest gift, of only six itemized bequests, amounted to a mere 10 *lire*, and the dowries bequeathed to his three daughters were extraordinarily small – a florin a piece.[108]

(For an illustration of a fourteenth-century *predella*, see Figure 8)

At the beginning of the fifteenth century, a man identified only by a single patronymic from the mountain village of Cerreto, northeast of Spoleto, exceeded the simple call for a burial portrait at the feet of the Virgin. He ordered 'the figure of Saint George with [his name inscribed] above his head, the Virgin Mary and Child in her arms', and the testator's father kneeling at her feet, holding a trumpet in one hand and in the other, flying a flag bearing the arms of the Orlandi family.[109] Why the Orlandi's arms were to be painted is not explained. Might the commissioner or his father have been a dependent of this Perugian noble family? Little attention has been paid to portraits of donor figures in the Trecento, especially ones commissioned by non-elites. In his famous essay on portraiture, Aby Warburg in one paragraph sails from Giotto's depiction of the kneeling donors in the Bardi chapel frescoes (*c.* 1325) to Francesco Sassetti's commission to Ghirlandaio in Santa Trinita, roughly 160 years later (Warburg, 1966: 114–15). Enrico Castelnuovo adds only the work of Simone Martini in Avignon to the description of Giotto's donor portraits before discussing more fully examples from the second half of the

---

[107] ASF, *Dipl.*, Olivetani di Arezzo, 1348 (day and month, unspecified).
[108] ASF, *Notarile antecosimiano* [hereafter, Not. antecos.], 5880, 131r, 23 August 1371.
[109] Archivio di Stato di Perugia [hereafter, ASPr], *Notarile Protocolli,* 22, 110r–v, 26 June 1400.

Figure 4 *Christ bearing the Cross with a Dominican Friar*, attributed to Barna da Siena (*c*.1350), The Frick Collection, New York. Wikimedia Commons.

Quattrocento (Castelnuovo, 1973). Other well-known works of art history similarly concentrate on the fifteenth and sixteenth centuries (Pope-Hennessey, 1966; Alazard, 1968; Gilbert, 1968; Pope-Hennessey & Christiansen, 1980; Hughes, 1986; Campbell, 1990; Christiansen & Weppelmann, 2011: 56–63). By contrast, my initial samples from last wills and testaments suggest that the desire for painted portraits in sacred scenes commissioned for ecclesiastical spaces flourished during the fourteenth century, and especially from non-elite donors. Of seventy-four commissions for stand-alone panel paintings or frescoes in my samples, fourteen testators ordered their portraits to be painted (and occasionally accompanied with further portraits of family ancestors), just

Figure 5 *Mary Magdalene with the Donor, Teobaldo Pontano*, 1320s.
Giotto. Magdalen Chapel, Lower Church, San Francesco, Assisi.
Wikimedia Commons.

under 20 per cent of the commissions in my samples. Most often, the donors demanded to be genuflecting at the feet of their patron saint or the Virgin Mary.

The earliest example of a commissioned portrait in my samples comes in 1315 from a Pisan testator, a recent émigré from north of the Alps. The German (*theotonicus*) Guarnerius f.q. Borlandi from the city of Liège (*Leggi*), a mercenary of the Pisan commune (*ad servitium et soldatum Pisis comunis*),

Figure 6 *Madonna and Child with Saint Catherine of Siena and a Carthusian Donor*, 1411–24. Metropolitan Museum, Robert Lehman Collection, 1975.

ordered a painting in the church of the hospital of Saint Clare, 'a beautiful and good image and figure of Our Lord Jesus Christ, the glorious and ever virgin Mary his mother, and other saints of God' to be chosen by the mercenary's executor, who was the prior of the hospital. The testator then instructed that he was to be represented genuflecting in front of the holy images (*et mei ipsius existentis genuflexi in ea*).[110] Another example from Pisa comes from a village in its hinterland. Gadduccius f.q. Beneciveni of San Piero ad Maccadium

---

[110] Archivio di Stato di Pisa, 72r–v, Ospedale di S. Chiara, no. 18, 31 January 1315.

Figure 7 *Saint Catherine of Alexandria disputing and two donors*, 1380.
Cenni di Francesco di Ser Cenni. Metropolitan Museum.

(*Macadio*) in the Valdiserchi, north of Pisa, was less precise than the German mercenary. His testament of 1334 left 12 *lire* 'to make' a panel painting that included 'his figure' to be placed at the altar of the village church.[111]

In the last decades of the Trecento, further non-elite testators sought lasting memory by insisting that their figures be included in their commissioned compositions. In 1382 the Aretine citizen Ceccus f.q. Vive Angeli Pieri

---

[111] ASF, *Not. antecos.,* n. 7575, 246v, 6 December 1335.

Figure 8 Predella of *The Coronation of the Virgin and Saints*, 1394. Giovanni di Tano Fei. Metropolitan Museum. Gift of Robert Lehman, 1950.

Figure 9 Madonna and Child with Two Donors, 1315–30. Goodhart
Ducciesque Master. Robert Lehman Collection, 1975.

commissioned for the plebis church of Arezzo a painting of the yet to be
canonized saint, Saint [sic] Nicholas of Tolentino, 'and at his feet the image
of [the testator's] own person'.[112] In 1390, the Perugian Johanna f.q. Ser Stefani
from Artimino, widow of the spice-trader Andrea and presently wife of Pauli
Petri Rubei, ordered a chapel to be built in Perugia's Servite church. 'In the

---

[112] ASF, *Dipl.*, *Misericordia di Arezzo*, 6 April 1382.

wall', above the altar, the annunciation was to be painted with 'the person of the testatrix and the said late Andrea her husband'.[113] In 1393, a Florentine parishioner of San Lorenzo ordered his executors to have painted 'honorably and well' Anthony the Abbot in the church of that 'blessed one', along with 'the image of the testator genuflecting'.[114] Yet the commission most obsessed with preserving a testator's earthly memory comes from a woman, the Perugian widow of Angeli Ser Celloli. After leaving all her landed possessions 'large and small' for the building and endowment of a 'covered' chapel called Santa Maria della Annuptiata in the Olivetani church of Monte Morciano, she commissioned 'a large and beautiful' panel painting for her chapel. It was 'to depict the figure or image of the Blessed Maria della Annuptiata with the Blessed Apostles, Peter and Paul, one on the right, the other on the left'. Then, 'somewhere else' in the composition, a figure 'in the likeness (*ad similitudinem*) of the testatrix's person' was to be painted with her coats of arms. These, she demanded, were to be exhibited 'for her true memory (*sue memorie in veritate*) and the commemoration of her soul'.[115] After 1400, such commissions from non-elites vanish almost completely from my samples, just when the prosperity of non-elites was steadily increasing absolutely and relative to elites.[116]

While the above-mentioned testators may not have been impoverished, they were not patrician elites. None possessed a family name, was identified as a merchant, belonged to an upper-guild profession, or was recognized by any title. Moreover, several cases show the economic heights to which artisans and shopkeepers could ascend by the 1360s. In 1361 an Aretine ironmonger[117] left the entirety of his residual estate to build a chapel in that city's Augustinian church, and in 1416 a cobbler from Vinci, who earlier worked in Florence's poorer parishes *sopr'Arno*, left 50 florins to construct a chapel to commemorate his remains in his native village. It was to be adorned with a panel painting, depicting the Virgin and 'the Blessed Saints John the Baptist, the Apostle Paul, Michael the Archangel and Anthony'.[118] Although 50 florins was at the bottom end of amounts to finance construction of a chapel even in a village church, as seen in my samples before 1425, the cobbler's expenditure was twenty times the average amount artisans spent on commissioning burial paintings alone. The

---

[113] ASPr, *Notarile Bastadelli*, no. 11, 74v–77r, 13 July 1390.

[114] ASF, *Not. antecos.*, n. 12064, 16r–v, 12 July 1393.

[115] ASPr, *Pergamene*, Mt. Morcino, no. 228, 4 March 1389.

[116] For examples of donor portraits from the fourteenth and early fifteenth century, see Figures 4–7 and 9.

[117] In late medieval Tuscany, an ironmonger was a craftsman or a small shopkeeper, and in Florence, a minor guildsman.

[118] ASF, Dipl., Archivio Generale, 13 October 1416.

cobbler, however, had not overreached the possibilities for post–Black Death artisans or their widows. In 1390, the widow of a belt-maker commissioned a chapel to be constructed in the ancient Aretine abbey of Santa Fiora.[119] In 1411, the widow of a tanner ordered the building of a chapel in Perugia's friary of Monte Morciano.[120] And in 1348, the Aretine widow of a weaver (in Florentine Tuscany, a disenfranchised worker without rights of citizenship) sold all her possessions for one pious bequest: the construction of a chapel in Arezzo's Santa Maria in Gradibus.[121]

To explain the rise of the artisan patrons, my argument hinged initially on economics: the shift in wealth spurred by the demographic catastrophe of plagues from 1348 through the early Renaissance buttressed these expenditures. But further investigation revealed that the economic relationship was the opposite of what I had expected. Instead, the commissions from peasants, artisans, and shopkeepers found in my sample of 2,879 testaments, drawn from archives in five cities and their regional hinterlands – Arezzo, Assisi, Florence, Perugia, and Pisa – do not suddenly increase during the post–Black Death century of increasing prosperity and equality.[122] Instead, these commissions rose through the first half of the fourteenth century and peaked with the Black Death in 1348. Then, when the economies of Tuscany and Umbria reversed gears around 1380 with textile production rebounding and silk manufacturing on the rise, improving conditions in the countryside, and the growth of new luxury goods,[123] artisan commissions declined and by the opening decades of the Quattrocento had virtually collapsed (Figure 10). Between 1401 and 1425, across all five city-states, only two artisan commissioners appear in my samples. When we turn to testamentary commissions of a grey area of non-elites (those not identified as peasants, workers, and artisans or by elite occupations, titles, or family names), the significance of the post-1375 era becomes more striking. From the Black Death until 1376, the percentages of artistic commissions to ecclesiastical institutions made by these non-elite testators continued rising. However, when prosperity and equality began to advance more sharply and steadily at the turn of the fifteenth century, their commissions dipped as steeply as those ordered by peasants or artisans (Figures 10 and 11).[124]

---

[119] Archivio Capitolare, Arezzo, Testamenta Ser Johanne Cecchi, 3r, 6 January 1389.

[120] ASPr, Pergamene, Monte Morciano, 335, 29 July 1411.

[121] ASF, Not. antecos., 20833, n.p., 11 July 1348.

[122] My samples in *The Cult of Remembrance* (Cohn, 1992) comprised six cities, totalling 3,226 testaments. For the present study, I was unable to retrieve evidence from Siena I collected in the early 1980s, because of corrupted computer files.

[123] See Section 2.

[124] The numbers of commissions were calculated by testators who instructed at least one commission and by the total number of commissions within a time period. Testators who made more

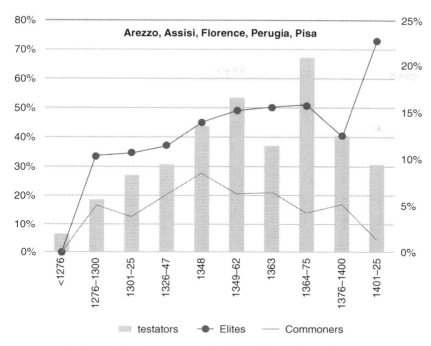

Figure 10 Testamentary Art Commissions 1276–1425.

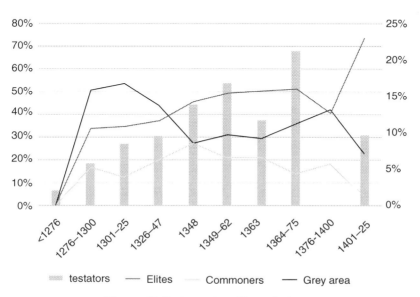

Figure 11 Testamentary Commissions.

To compose Figures 10 and 11, various terms were defined operationally. First, 'art' is defined as requests to construct (a) chapels,[125] monumental graves,[126] monasteries, churches, or hospitals; (b) paintings which described figures and details of a composition; (c) priestly vestments, altar cloths, grave-stones, coats of arms, candles, and candle holders, but only if figures were specified. Second, 'elites' are classified as ones with family names or titles 'Dominus' ('Messer') or 'Ser' (unless a parish priest), and *iudex, canonicus, mercator*, and other upper-guild professions, including their daughters, wives, and widows. Third, commoners are identified as those with craft occupations and trades, or ones residing in villages and identified only by a single patronymic. Testators of the grey region were those without either elite or commoner designations. They decrease from comprising more than 50 per cent of the testators before 1325 to 23 per cent by 1401–25. The left y-axis of these graphs indicates the percentages of commissioners according to social category; the right y-axis, the percentage of testators in a given period and of a social category commissioning these artworks. I have used percentages instead of raw numbers because of variations in the numbers of testators for each of the ten chronological periods. The raw numbers divided by city-state, period, and social category are presented in Tables 1 and 2.

Explanations

The early Renaissance did not, however, mark a general decline in artistic commissions to churches, hospitals, and monasteries. For elites – identified by family names, titles of nobility, and upper-guild professions – the last fifty years of my analysis (1376 to 1425) registered a sharp rise in their commissions.[127] They now dominated ecclesiastic art commissions. Effectively, peasants, artisans, and shopkeepers had lost their earlier privileges to commemorate themselves and their ancestors visually in ecclesiastical spaces. The price of art appears as a fundamental lever, creating the scissors graphic, that widened the gap between elites and commoners. By the beginning of the fifteenth century, the price for ecclesiastical commissions skyrocketed,

---

than one commission came exclusively from elites or the grey area of non-elites. The two trends, however, appear much the same (see Tables 1 and 2).

[125] When referring to bequests of chapels, I have limited it to the construction of chapels in contrast to altars, and when phrases 'to construct' are explicit, such as with aedificare, facere (fieri cappellam), construatur, etc.

[126] On the numerous tomb slabs of various types that survive in Florentine churches commissioned in the fourteenth and fifteenth centuries, see Butterfield, 1994.

[127] In addition, see Goldthwaite, 1993: 121–9, who without numbers maintains that the demand for art in ecclesiastic institutions soared in Italy and especially in fifteenth-century Florence, propelled by the wealth of mercantile elites.

Table 1 Artistic Commissioners by City-State 1276–1425

City-States	Testaments	Commissions	Elites	Commoners	Grey Area (Non-elites)
Arezzo	616	112	61	21	30
Assisi	258	18	2	2	14
Florence	647	94	49	13	32
Perugia	574	59	22	12	25
Pisa	784	70	31	13	26
Total	2879	353	165	61	127

Table 2 Artistic Commissions by City-State 1276–1425

City-State	Testaments	Commissions	Elites	Commoners	Grey Area (Non-elites)
Arezzo	616	165	99	25	41
Assisi	258	24	4	2	18
Florence	647	127	71	16	40
Perugia	574	69	27	12	30
Pisa	784	97	48	11	38
Total	2879	487	249	66	172

rising nine times over what it had averaged during the previous generation, and a fantastic twenty-six times over what it fetched in the 1360s, despite the period 1375–1475 being deflationary as far as basic commodities can be measured (Cohn, 1992, 266–8).

These prices, however, do not reflect what individual paintings of comparable materials, dimensions, and artistic prestige might have demanded.[128] Rather, to gain artistic space in ecclesiastical buildings the bar had risen to extraordinary heights: a complex of items now appears to have been necessary. After 1380, the chances of leaving lasting memorials in churches rested increasingly on large donations for constructing burial chapels that included bequests of silver chalices, priestly vestments, altars, sculpted monumental tombs, elaborate fresco cycles, and livings for priests to sing perpetual masses. A structural change in the possibilities of commissioning explains the price rise. Single gifts of inexpensive panel paintings, not belonging to such grandiose chapel complexes, had nearly disappeared from testamentary commissions no matter who the donor happened to be. In fact, of these various accoutrements to personal and family fame, the paintings, when monetized, were often the least expensive of the items.

This early Renaissance reversal of non-elites as art patrons paralleled their political losses. Not only in Florence after the defeat of the Ciompi but also across regions of Europe, a paradox emerged: as artisans' real wages began to increase in some places and for certain occupations from the 1360s and in others by the early fifteenth century, their political status declined, with losses in guild and citizen rights and office holding and election to large legislative assemblies in Italy. Their loss of power to commission works in ecclesiastic spaces to memorialize themselves, their ancestors, and their places of burial with works of art reflects another dimension to non-elites' decline in status during the Renaissance.[129] These losses in artistic and spiritual representation were connected to their political losses, and evolved in relation to both their perceived economic gains immediately after the Black Death and real gains in wealth later in the century. In cooperation with ecclesiastic institutions, often headed by members of the same oligarchic families, secular elites were able to confront threatening rises of economic equality and artisan prosperity created by the new demographic realities. In their defence, elites turned to other spheres to preserve and then to widen their social distinction.

To substantiate these hypotheses, testamentary samples must be extended, geographically and temporally. Moreover, new questions can be asked. What mechanisms did elites devise to create their virtual monopolies within

---

[128] On factors determining prices of pictures and prices for pictorial art over time, see O'Malley, 2005.

[129] For northern and central Italy, a similar decline can be seen in popular protest from the 1370s; Cohn, 2006: 225–7.

ecclesiastic institutions to commission art and celebrate their lives and those of
their ancestors at the expense of those beneath them? And how did non-elites
react to closures for their spiritual and aesthetic space? For the second question,
at least three pathways appear to have arisen. First, commissions for sacred art
in non-elites' homes and shops may have increased, as suggested by the account
books of the painter Neri di Bicci. However, instead of commissions that
allowed artisans choices over the subjects or figures they wished to be included
or their judgements on compositions, a number of these were 'sold (vendei)' by
Neri, ready-made for purchase, and, unlike the earlier commissioned works in
sacred places, I have found none that describe the commissioners or their
ancestors portrayed at the feet of chosen patron saints (Holmes, 2003; D.V.
Kent, 2000: 111–16; Neri di Bicci, 1976).[130] Second, non-elites turned to
cheaper, more ephemeral votive offerings, which increased in number through
the fifteenth century, cramming the aisles of pilgrimage churches and other
specialized churches such as Florence's Santissima Annunciata. These objects
also were seldom commissioned, at least by artisans or peasants, but purchased
from shops (Holmes, 2011; Jacobs, 2013). Third, and most importantly, during
the fifteenth century and through the early modern period, artisans and other
non-elites pooled their resources through their guilds and more often their
religious confraternities to commission collectively more costly altarpieces,
often by notable artists, which could compete for sacred space under the new
ecclesiastic priorities and aesthetics of the fifteenth century (Bent, 2016: 24;
Humfrey & MacKenney, 1986; Seidel, 1994; Trexler, 1980: 68–9; Wisch &
Ahl, 2000).[131] Yet the extent to which these commissions reflected individual
artisans' aesthetics or decisions about subjects and compositions is another
matter, and I know none of them to portray individual artisans or name them
for posterity. Finally, no one has plotted the course of any of these alternative
trends or connected them to artisan losses in status during the post–Black Death
century.

In conclusion, non-elite patronage of chapels, altars, and burial paintings that
could include commissions from peasants and disenfranchised labourers
increased during the first half of the fourteenth century and through the horrific
months of the Black Death in 1348. This art patronage, however, declined
during the second half of the century, especially in the final quarter, and by
the fifteenth century it had virtually disappeared – not because of a decline in
non-elites' economic well-being, but for the opposite reason. The abrupt change

---

[130] Neri di Bicci, *Le ricordanze*.
[131] On civic committees judging competition for public projects, as with Florence's baptismal
doors in 1420, see Haines, 1989. By the fifteenth century, however, these were composed almost
exclusively of merchants and upper guildsmen.

in the supply of labour sparked by the Black Death and successive plagues spurred elites to engineer new non-economic means to extend their status and privileges. One arena of this elite reaction was art patronage in sacred places. In the opening years of the fifteenth century, magnate families such as Florence's Frescobaldi and wealthy merchants such as Arezzo's Bracci offered hundreds, even thousands, of florins to build complex burial chapels, embellished with expensive fresco cycles and livings to priests to sing perpetual masses for these families' salvation, but only if churches agreed to prevent others later impinging on these spaces.[132] The demands of a 'Probus Vir' in Florence in 1417 went further. His founding and decoration of a chapel in 1417 in Santo Spirito for his family tomb, with sculpted coats of arms, paintings, stained glass, and livings for priests, were conditional on Santo Spirito's Augustinian friars promising to prohibit any banners, plates, arms, or paintings that would block the view of his chapel from as far away as the church's organ.[133] The new demands of these early fifteenth-century merchant elites suggest that the white-washing of church interiors and stripping of cheap column paintings, plates, and burial monuments that artisans had earlier commissioned to preserve their own memories began at least a century before Cosimo I and Giorgio Vasari transfigured Florence's ecclesiastic interiors in the mid-sixteenth century to conform to what then was imagined as the aesthetics of ancient Greek temples (Hall, 1979). As early as 1429 the Commune of Florence imposed a tax on families who possessed chapels and tombs in churches for the purposes of ornamenting and white-washing church walls (Moisé, 1845: 73). Two decades later, Leon Batista Alberti in *De re aedificatoria* expressed similar doctrines for a new Renaissance ecclesiastic aesthetic. For him, 'the walls of the ideal church interior' should be predominantly white (Hills, 1990). At the same time, Pope Pius II, in his *Commentaries*, commanded: 'No one shall deface the whiteness of the walls and the columns. No one shall draw pictures. No one shall hang up pictures. No one shall erect more chapels and altars than there are at present.' According to Henk van Os, evidence from Sienese church interiors shows that Pius's desires were being carried out (van Os, 1987).[134] Further investigation of municipal decrees, church synods, and church inventories would uncover further examples. These would enable historians to chart clearer trajectories

---

[132] On Lazzaro Bracci's testament of 1410, his commissions, and conflict with the Franciscans, see Cohn, 1992: 151–2 and 312; and Borsook, 1980: 92–3.

[133] ASF, *Dipl.*, Archivio Generale, 19 June 1417.

[134] Wackernagel, 1938, called this cleansing of ecclesiastical space from the clutter of column paintings and other small works of art 'the spirit of a new Renaissance ideal' (242). Yet, despite this cleansing, Wackernagel concluded: 'Only this much might still be added: the general artistic conditions of the Renaissance period in Florence were fundamentally determined by the existence of an uncommonly strong, multifaceted demand for art and an equally extensive

of authorities' actions to restrict new commissions for less expensive works of art in ecclesiastic buildings and to destroy earlier ones commissioned by non-elites for their everlasting remembrance.[135]

General Conclusions

By the mid-fifteenth century, a new Renaissance aesthetic grounded in supposed notions of pristine Greek temples came of age, a century before Vasari became Cosimo I's supervisor of public works and the interiors of medieval churches began to be transformed on a colossal scale. The impetus for this new aesthetic and destruction of what previously had hung or had been frescoed on those white-washed walls began two centuries before the Florentine Grand Duchy. It grew not simply from attempts to recover ancient aesthetics but from social psychology, the consequences of the Black Death and plagues of the late fourteenth century, which by the fifteenth century transformed the value of labour not only of the unskilled, but of middling groups of highly skilled artisans, shopkeepers, and even petty merchants. Threatened with rising economic equality, elites sought ways to preserve their class 'distinction'.[136]

Traces of this psychological history would endure through the early modern period in Italy. One mechanism, not discussed herein, concerned property law and is central to the testaments themselves. Changes in inheritance practices – *fideicommissum* clauses – increased in frequency in Tuscan testaments during the fifteenth century and spread from the aristocracy to merchant elites. These channelled property down male lines from one generation to the next to block alienation of landed properties and city palaces, thereby keeping estates intact to preserve family wealth and entrench wealth inequality (Cohn, 1992, ch. 5). As Guido Alfani, Di Tullio, and Murphy have argued, these mechanisms were slow to penetrate urban elites after the Black Death. However, by the time of the next major demographic shock – the plagues of 1629–33 in northern cities such as Milan and Venice – they had become diffused, providing legal buffers to dampen the effects of sudden changes in the supply of labour, which almost

---

body of patrons, encompassing all social levels.' However, he provides no statistics to substantiate this claim, not even examples of any artisan patrons or others further down the social ladder than those with prominent Florentine family names.

[135] See, for instance, the actions of the fifteenth-century parish priest in the Florentine Mugello, who whitewashed all the frescoes in his church that he judged as ugly (*Motti e Facezie*, 1995; Trexler, 1972: 28). On later visitations and removal of church paintings, see the new form of Counter-Reformation inquisitions (*visite*), as with Francesco Bossi's for Siena in 1575–6; Archivio Arcivescovile di Siena, *Visite*, no. 26; and Cohn, 1988: 186–8.

[136] For the now classic theoretical work on social and artistic distinction, see Bourdieu, 1979. Also, on this motive in general during the Italian Renaissance, see Nelson and Zeckhauser, 2008: ch. 3.

three centuries earlier had underpinned a major redistribution of wealth (Alfani & Di Tullio, 2019, ch. 2; Alfani & Murphy, 2017).[137]

For the post–Black Death century, the mechanisms were less direct. The onslaughts were on workers' and citizens' rights in their guilds and participation in legislative assemblies in the transformation of Italian city-state governments from communes to patrician oligarchies or domination by princely families. As shown in Section 2, this narrowing of government swept through republics such as Lucca, Siena, Florence, and Venice, along with territorial states traditionally labelled 'despotic', such as Milan, Perugia, and Bologna.[138] These shifts in power and prestige have been the subject of many studies but have generally focused on politics and individual Italian cities in isolation. Research has yet to analyse this decline in artisan power and prestige that promoted strengthening vertical ties at the expense of horizontal class relations within the wider context of the Black Death catastrophe. Certainly, as Sections 1 and 2 illustrate, the chronologies of these developments differed from place to place. Historians, however, have yet to frame these developments of political inequality as arising from the post–Black Death context of increasing economic equality.

Finally, this Element has found a third trend. Unlike political developments, it is presently *terra incognita* and marks a second paradox against the backdrop of rising economic equality and non-elite prosperity. In this sphere, the sudden post-plague psychological need for elite distinction spurred a driving cultural inequality that underlies the increased expenditures in artistic creativity and buttressed the Renaissance in art production. Threatened by rising economic equality, elites devised ways to curtail commissions for sacred art from non-elites that previously had marked their spiritual and earthly remembrance. A major plank of this restructuring of artistic creation privileged elaborate projects of chapels, altarpieces, and paintings with extensive furnishings and livings to priests at the expense of small burial panels or *predella* that non-elites commissioned through the Trecento. This earlier world of public art is presently hidden from history, not so much due to the vagaries of time, weather, or war as through conscious elite restrictions, followed by its destruction throughout the Renaissance. The recovery of this cultural history and its origins in the early Renaissance relies on digging through tens of thousands of archival records – last wills and testaments. The intertwining of these paradoxes in economic, political, and cultural history has never before been examined for any period or place in history.

---

[137] Another mechanism was fiscal corruption and increases in exemptions, Alfani, 2010: 536–7 and 545; and Alfani and Di Tullio, 2019.

[138] On this false dichotomy in governmental geography, see Fantoni, 2020.

Bibliography

Archival Sources

Archivio Capitolare, Arezzo
  Testamenta

Archivio di Stato, Firenze
  Provvisioni
  Diplomatico
  Notarile antecosimiano

Archivio di Stato di Perugia
  Notarile Bastardelli
  Notarile Protocolli
  Pergamene

Archivio di Stato di Pisa
  Ospedale di S. Chiara

Archivio di Stato di Siena
  Visite

Primary Sources

Agnolo di Tura del Grasso, *Cronaca Senese attribuita ad Agnolo di Tura del Grasso detta la cronaca maggiore, [1300–1351]*, 252–564. In *Cronache Senesi . . .*, ed. A. Lisini and F. Iacometti, Rerum Italicarum Scriptores, XV/6.1. Città del Castello: Lapi, 1939.

Boccaccio, Giovanni. *Decameron*, ed. Vittore Branca. Milan: Arnoldo Mandadori editore, 1976.

Burigozzo, Gianmarco. *Cronica Milanese dal 1500 al 1544, con note*. Milano: La Libreria Ferrario, 1851:

Il contratto di mezzadria nella Toscana medievale. Vol 1: Contado di Siena, sec. XIII-1348, ed. Giuliano Pinto and Paolo Pirillo ; Vol. 2. *Contado di Firenze, secolo XIII*, ed. Oretta Muzzi and Maria Daniela Nenci ; and Vol. 3. *Contado di Siena, 1349–1518*, ed. Gabriella Piccinni, Fonti di storia toscana; 3–4, 6. Florence: Olschki, 1987–1992.

Cronaca di Vigevano, ossia dell'origine e principio di Vigevano . . . di Cesare Nubilonio, ed. Carlo Negroni, 205–386. In *Miscellanea di storia italiana*, XXIX (1891).

La Cronica perugina cinquecentesca di Giulio di Costantino, ed. Gaia Rossetti and Gina Scentoni. Spoleto: Centro italiano di Studi sull'alto medioevo, 1992.

Damião de Gois, *Chronica do felicissimo rey dom Emanuel da gloriosa memoria*. Lisbon: Aluarez, 1619.

Facezie e motti dei secoli XV e XVI. Codice inedito magliabecchiano, ed. G. Papanti. Bologna: Commissione per i testi de lingua, 1874.

Knighton, Henry. *Chronicon*, 75–80. In *The Black Death*, ed. Rosemary Horrox, Manchester medieval sources series. Manchester University Press, 1994.

Langland, William. *Piers the Ploughman*, trans. J.F. Goodridge. Harmondsworth, 1959.

Maqrīzī. *Al-sulūk li-ma 'rifat duwal al-mulūk*, trans. G. Wiet, 'La grande peste noire en Syrie et en Egypte', *Etudes d'orientalisme dédiées à la mémoire de Lévi-Provençal*, I. Paris, 1962, 367–80.

Marx, Karl. *Capital*, trans. Ben Fowkes, The Marx Library, 3 vols. New York: Vintage Books, 1976.

Mémoires de Pierre de Fenin, comprenant le récit des événements qui se sont passés en France et en Bourgogne sous les règnes de Charles VI et Charles VII (1407–1427), ed. Mlle. DuPont, Société de l'histoire de France. Paris: Renouard, 1837.

Il Memoriale di Iacopo di Coluccino Bonavia Medico Lucchese (1373–1416), ed. Pia Pittino Calamari. In *Studi di Filologia Italiana*, 24. Florence, 1966.

Motti e Facezie del Piovano Arlotto, ed. Gianfranco Folena. Milan: Ricciardi, 1995.

Neri di Bicci, *Le ricordanze (10 marzo 1453 – 24 aprile 1475)*, ed. Bruno Santi. Pisa: Marlin, 1976.

Le novella di Gentile Sermini da Siena, ed. F. Vigo. Livorno: Vigo, 1874.

Sacchetti, Franco. *Il Trecentonovelle*, ed. Antonio Lanza. Florence: Sansoni, 1984.

Sanudo, Marin. *I diarii di Marino Sanuto*, ed. Rinaldo Fulin, Federico Stefani, Nicolò Barozzi, et al., 58 vols. Venice: R. Deputazione venta di storia patria, 1879–1903.

'Sumptuary Legislation, 1363', 340–2. In *The Black Death*, ed. Rosemary Horrox, Manchester medieval sources series. Manchester University Press, 1994.

Stefani, Marchionne di Coppo. *Cronica fiorentina*, ed. Niccolò Rodolico, Rerum Italicarum Scriptores, XXX/1. Città di Castello: S. Lapi, 1903.

Villani, Matteo. *Cronica con la continuazione di Filippo Villani*, ed. Giuseppe Porta, 2 vols. Parma: Fondazione Pietro Bembo, 1995.

Secondary Sources

Ady, Cecilia. (1937). *The Bentivoglio of Bologna: A Study in Depotism*. Oxford University Press.

Alfani, Guido. (2015). 'Economic Inequality in Northwestern Italy: A Long-term View (Fourteenth to Eighteenth Centuries)', *Journal of Economic History*, 75: 1058–96.

Alfani, Guido. (2021). 'Economic Inequality in Preindustrial Times: Europe and Beyond', *Journal of Economic Literature*, 59: 3–44.

Alfani, Guido. (2010). 'Wealth Inequalities and Population Dynamics in Early Modern Northern Italy', *Journal of Interdisciplinary History*, 40: 513–49.

Alfani, Guido and Francesco Ammannati. (2017). 'Long-term Trends in Economic Inequality: The Case of the Florentine State, ca. 1300–1800', *Economic History Review* 70: 1072–102.

Alfani, Guido and Tommy Murphy. (2017). 'Plague and Lethal Epidemics in the Pre-Industrial World', *Journal of Economic History* 77: 314–43.

Alfani, Guido and Marco Percoco. (2019). 'Plague and Long-term Development: The Lasting Effects of the 1629–30 Epidemic on Italian Cities', *Economic History Review*, 72: 1175–201.

Alfani, Guido and Matteo Di Tullio. (2019). *The Lion's Share. Inequality and the Rise of the Fiscal State in Preindustrial Europe*. Cambridge University Press.

Alfani, Guido and Wouter Ryckbosch. (2016). 'Growing Apart in Early Modern Europe? A Comparison of Inequality Trends in Italy and the Low Countries, 1500–1800', *Explorations in Economic History* 62: 143–53.

Alazard, Jean. (1968). *The Florentine Portrait*, trans. Barbara Whelpton. New York: Schocken Books.

Allen, Robert C. (2001). 'The Great Divergence in European Wages and Prices from the Middle Ages to the First World War', *Explorations in Economic History*, 38: 411–47.

Ammannati, Francesco. (2015). 'La Peste Nera e la distribuzione della proprietà nella Lucchesia del tardo medioevo', *Popolazione e Storia*, 2: 21–45.

Aston, T.H. and C.H.E. Philpin (eds) (1985). *The Brenner Debate: Agrarian Class Structure and Economic Development in Pre-Industrial Europe*. Cambridge University Press.

Bacci, Michele. (2000). *'Pro remedio animae': Immagini sacre e pratiche devozionali in Italia centrale (secoli XIII e XIV)*. Pisa: GISEM – edizioni ETS.

Bailey, Mark. (2014). *The Decline of Serfdom in Late Medieval England: From Bondage to Freedom*. Woodbridge: Boydell.

Barron, Caroline. (2004). 'The Political Culture of Medieval London'. In Linda Clark and Christian Carpenter, eds. *Political Culture in Late Medieval Britain*, The Fifteenth Century, 4. Woodbridge: Boydell, 111–33.

Barron, Caroline. (1990). 'Ralph Holland and the London Radicals, 1438–1444'. In Richard Holt and Gervase Rosser, eds. *The English Medieval Town: A Reader in English Urban History, 1200–1540*. London: Longman, 160–83.

Bec, Christian. (1981). 'Le paysan dans la nouvelle toscane (1350–1530)'. In *Civiltà ed economia agricola in Toscana nei secc. XIII-XV: Problemi della vita delle campagne nel tardo medioevo (Pistoia, 21–24 aprile 1977)*. Pistoia: Centro italiano di studi di storia e d'arte, 29–52.

Benadusi, Giovanna. (1996). *A Provincial Elite in Early Modern Tuscany: Family and Power in the Creation of the State*. Baltimore: Johns Hopkins University Press.

Bent, George R. (2016). *Public Art and Visual Culture in Early Republican Florence*. Cambridge University Press.

Blockmans, Wim. (1980). 'The Social and Economic Effects of Plague 1349–1500', *Revue Belge*, 58: 833–63.

Bois, Guy. (1976). *Crise du féodalisme: économie et démographie en Normandie du début du 14e siècle au milieu du 16e siècle*. Paris: Presses de la Fondation Nationale des Sciences Politiques.

Borsook, Eve. (1980). *The Mural Painters of Tuscany from Cimabue to Andrea del Sarto*, 2nd ed. Oxford University Press.

Bourdieu, Pierre. (2010). *Distinction: A Social Critique of the Judgement of Taste*, trans Richard Nice. London: Routledge [original in French, 1979].

Bowd, Stephen. (2018). *Renaissance Mass Murder: Civilians and Soldiers during the Italian Wars*. Oxford University Press.

Brenner, Robert. (1976). 'Agrarian Class Structure and Economic Development in Pre-Industrial Europe', *Past & Present*, 70: 30–75.

Bresc, Henri. (1986). *Un monde méditerranéen: economie et société en Sicile, 1300–1450*, 2 vols. Rome: École française de Rome.

Brown, Alison. (1994). 'Lorenzo and Public Opinion in Florence: The Problem of Opposition'. In Gian Carlo Garfagnini, ed. *Lorenzo il Magnifico e il suo mondo: Convegno internazionale di studi (Firenze 9–13 giugno 1992)*. Florence: Olschki, 61–85.

Brown, Judith. (1982). *In the Shadow of Florence: Provincial Society in Renaissance Pescia*. New York: Oxford University Press.

Brucker, Gene. (1977). *The Civic World of Early Renaissance Florence*. Princeton University Press.

Brucker, Gene. (1983). *Renaissance Florence*, 2nd ed. Berkeley: University of California Press.

Butterfield, Andrew. (1994). 'Social Structure and the Typology of Funerary Monuments in Early Renaissance Florence', *RES: Anthropology and Aesthetics*, 26: 47–67.

Caferro, William. (2018). *Petrarch's War: Florence and the Black Death in Context*. Cambridge University Press.

Campbell, Bruce and Mark Overton. (1993). 'A New Perspective on Medieval and Early Modern Agriculture: Six Centuries of Norfolk Farming c. 1250–c.1850', *Past & Present*, 141: 38–105.

Campbell, Lorne. (1990). *Renaissance Portraits: European Portrait-painting in the 14th, 15th, and 16th Centuries*. New Haven: Yale University

Cannon, Joanna. (2013). *Religious Poverty, Visual Riches: Art in the Dominican Churches of Central Italy in the Thirteenth and Fourteenth Centuries*. New Haven: Yale University Press.

Caracausi, Andrea. (2018). 'I salari'. In Renata Ago, ed., *Storia del lavoro in Italia. Vol. III: L'età moderna: Trasformazioni e risorse del lavoro tra associazioni di mestiere e pratiche individuali*. Rome: Castelvecchi, 103–33.

Casini, Bruno. (1983). 'Note sul potere di acquisto dei salari a Pisa nei primi anni della Signoria gambacortiana'. In *Studi in onore di Leopoldo Sandri*, 3 vols. Rome: Ministero per i beni culturali e ambientali, I, 227–75.

Castelnuovo, Enrico. (1973). 'Il significato del ritratto pittorico nella società'. In Ruggiero Romanao and Corrado Vivanti, eds. *Storia d'Italia*. V: *Documenti*. Turin: Einaudi, 1035–94.

Chojnacki, Stanley. (1994). 'Social Identity in Renaissance Venice: The Second Serrata', *Renaissance Studies* 8: 341–58.

Christiansen, Keith and Stefan Weppelmann (eds) (2011). *The Renaissance Portrait: From Donatello to Bellini*. New York: The Metropolitan Museum of Art.

Clark, Gregory. (2007). 'The Long March of History: Farm Wages, Population, and Economic Growth, England 1209–1869', *Economic History Review*, 60: 97–135.

Cognasso, Francesco (1955a). 'Il Ducato Visconteo da Gian Galeazzo a Filippo Maria'. *Storia di Milano*, VI: *Il Ducato e la repubblica ambrosiana (1392–1450)*. Milan: Fondazione Treccani degli Alfieri, 21–106.

Cognasso, Francesco (1955b). 'La repubblica di S. Ambrogio'. In *Storia di Milano*, VI: *Il Ducato e la repubblica ambrosiana (1392–1450)*. Milan: Fondazione Treccani degli Alfieri, 387–452.

Cohn, Jr, Samuel (2007). 'After the Black Death: Labour Legislation and Attitudes Towards Labour in Late-medieval Western Europe', *Economic History Review*, 60, 3: 457–485.

Cohn, Jr, Samuel (1999). *Creating the Florentine State: Peasants and Rebellion, 1348–1434*. Cambridge University Press.

Cohn, Jr, Samuel (1992). *The Cult of Remembrance and the Black Death: Six Renaissance Cities in Central Italy*. Baltimore: Johns Hopkins University Press.

Cohn, Jr, Samuel (1988). *Death and Property in Siena: Strategies for the Afterlife, 1205–1800*. Baltimore: Johns Hopkins University Press.

Cohn, Jr. Samuel (2018). *Epidemics: Hate and Compassion from the Plague of Athens to AIDS*. Oxford University Press.

Cohn, Jr, Samuel (2009). 'Highlands and Lowlands in Late Medieval Tuscany'. In Dauvit Broun and Martin MacGregor, eds. *Mìorun Mòr nan Gall, 'The Great Ill-Will of the Lowlander'?: Lowland Perceptions of the Highlands, Medieval and Modern*. Glasgow: Centre for Scottish and Celtic Studies, 110–27.

Cohn, Jr., Samuel (2006). *Lust for Liberty: The Politics of Social Revolt in Medieval Europe, 1200–1425*. Cambridge, MA: Harvard University Press.

Cohn, Jr, Samuel (2020). 'Material Culture without Objects: Artisan Artistic Commissions in Early Renaissance Italy'. In Rembrandt Duits, ed. *The Art of the Poor: The Aesthetic Material Culture of the Lower Classes in Europe, 1300–1600*. London: Bloomsbury Academic, 23–8 [text] and 203–7 [notes].

Cohn, Jr, Samuel (1996a). 'Piété et commande d'oeuvres d'art après la Peste Noire', *Annales: Histoire, Sciences sociales*, 51, 3: 551–73.

Cohn, Jr., Samuel (2021, forthcoming). *Popular Protest and Ideals of Democracy in Late Renaissance Italy*, Oxford University Press.

Cohn, Jr., Samuel (2013). *Popular Protest in Late Medieval English Towns*. Cambridge University Press.

Cohn, Jr, Samuel (2012). 'Renaissance attachment to things: Material Culture in Last Wills and Testaments', *Economic History Review*, 65, 3: 984–1004.

Cohn, Jr, Samuel (2016). 'Rich and Poor in Western Europe, c. 1375–1475: The Political Paradox of Material Well-Being'. In Sharon Farmer, ed. *Approaches to Poverty in Medieval Europe: Complexities, Contradictions, Transformations, c. 1100–1500*. Turnhout: Brepols, 145–73.

Cohn, Jr, Samuel (1996b). *Women in the Streets: Essays on Sex and Power in Renaissance Italy*. Baltimore: Johns Hopkins University Press.

Connell, William. (2000). *La città dei crucci: fazioni e clientele in uno stato repubblicano '400*. Florence: Nuova Toscana.

Damsholt, Thorben. (1964). 'Some Observations on Four Series of Tuscan Corn Prices, 1520–1630', *Scandinavian Economic History Review*, 12: 145–64.

de Vries, Jan. (1984), *European Urbanization, 1500–1800*. Cambridge, MA.: Harvard University Press.

Di Tullio, Matteo. (2011). *La ricchezza della comunità: guerra, risorse e cooperazione nella Geradadda del Cinquecento*. Venice: Marsilio.

Du Boulay F.R.H. (1970). *An Age of Ambition: English Society in the Late Middle Ages*. London: Nelson.

Dumolyn, Jan and Yelle Haemers. (2005). 'Patterns of Urban Rebellion in Medieval Flanders', *Journal of Medieval History*, 31: 369–93.

Dyer, Christopher. (1998). 'Did the Peasants Really Starve'. In Martha Carlin and Joel Rosenthal, ed. *Food and Eating in Medieval Europe*. London: Hambledon, 53–71.

Dyer, Christopher. (2002). *Making a Living in the Middle Ages: The People of Britain 850–1520*. New Haven: Yale University Press.

Dyer, Christopher. (2004). 'The Political Life of the Fifteenth-Century English Village'. In Linda Clark and Christian Carpenter, eds. *Political Culture in Late Medieval Britain: The Fifteenth Century*, 4, Woodbridge: Boydell, 135–58.

Dyer, Christopher. (2012). 'Poverty and its Relief in Late Medieval England', *Past & Present*, 216: 41–78.

Dyer, Christopher. (1984). 'The Social and Economic Background to the Rural Revolt of 1381'. In R.H. Hilton and T.H. Aston, eds. *The English Rising of 1381*. Cambridge University Press, 9–42.

Dyer, Christopher. (1989). *Standards of Living in the Later Middle Ages: Social Change in England c.1200–1520*. Cambridge University Press.

Dyer, Christopher. (1995). 'Taxation and Communities in Late Medieval England'. In Richard Britnell and John Hatcher, eds. *Progress and Problems in Medieval England: Essays in Honour of Edward Miller*. Cambridge University Press, 168–90.

Dyer, Christopher. (2000). 'Work Ethics in the Fourteenth Century'. In James Bothwell, P.J.P. Goldberg, and W.M. Ormrod, eds. *The Problem of Labour in Fourteenth-Century England*. Woodbridge: Boydell, 21–41.

Faith, Rosamond. (1981). 'The Class Struggle in Fourteenth Century England'. In R. Samuel, ed. *People's History and Socialist Theory*. London: Routledge & Kegan Paul, 50–60.

Fantoni, Marcello. (2020). 'Courts and Republics in Late Medieval and Renaissance Italy'. In Fabrizio Ricciardelli and Marcello Fantoni, eds. *Republicanism: A Theoretical and Historical Perspective*. Rome: Viella, 175–220.

Farmer, David (1988). 'Prices and Wages'. In H.E. Hallam, ed., *The Agrarian History of England and Wales*, vol. II, 1042–1350: 716–817.

Fochesato, Mattia. (2018). 'Origins of Europe's North–South Divide: Population Changes, Real Wages and the 'Little Divergence' in Early Modern Europe', *Explorations in Economic History*, 70: 91–131.

Franceschi, Franco. (1993). *Oltre il "Tumulto": I fiorentini dell'Arte della Lana fra Tre e Quattrocento Firenze*. Florence: Olschki.

Franceschi, Franco. (2013). 'Stoffa per ricchi, stoffa per diventare ricchi. Il boom della seta nel Quattrocento. In ' . . . *e seremo tutti ricchi': Lavoro, mobilità sociale e conflittti nella cità dell'italia medievale*. Pisa: Pacini, 53–68.

Freeman, Mark. (2008). *St Albans: A History*. Lancaster: Carnegie.

Fubini, Riccardo. (1991). 'From Social to Political Representation in Renaissance Florence'. In Anthony Molho, Kurt Raaflaub, and Julia Emlen, eds., *City-States in Classical Antiquity and Medieval Italy*. Stuttgart: Franz Steiner Verlag, 223–39.

Fubini, Riccardo. (1994). *Italia Quatrocentesca. Politica, diplomazia nell'età di Lorenzo il Magnifico*. Milan: Franco Angeli.

Gasquet, Francis Aidan (1893). *The Great Pestilence (AD 1348–9) Now Commonly Known as The Black Death*. London: Simpkin Marshall.

Gilbert, Creighton. (1968). 'The Renaissance Portrait', *Burlington Magazine*, 110: 278–85.

Goldthwaite, Richard. (1980). *The Building of Renaissance Florence: An Economic and Social History*. Baltimore: John Hopkins University Press.

Goldthwaite, Richard. (2009). *The Economy of Renaissance Florence*. Baltimore: Johns Hopkins University Press.

Goldthwaite, Richard. (1975). 'I prezzi del grano a Firenze dal XIV al XVI secolo', *Quaderni Storici*, 28: 15–36.

Goldthwaite, Richard. (1993). *Wealth and the Demand for Art in Italy 1300–1600*. Baltimore: Johns Hopkins University Press.

Grillo, Paolo. (2012). 'The Long Life of the Popolo of Milan: Revolts against the Visconti in the Fourteenth and Fifteenth Centuries'. In Samuel Cohn and Fabrizio Ricciadelli, eds. *The Culture of Violence in Renaissance Italy: Proceedings of the International Conference, Georgetown University at Villa Le Balze, 3–4 May 2010*. Florence: Le Lettere, 221–36.

Haemers, Yelle. (2009). 'Factionalism and State Power in the Flemish Revolt (1482–1492),' *Journal of Social History*, 42: 1009–39.

Haemers, Yelle. (2005): 'A Moody Community? Emotion and Ritual in Late Medieval Urban Revolts'. In Elodie Lecuppre-Desjardin and Anne-Laure Van Bruaene, eds. *Emotions in the Heart of the City (14th–16th century)*. Studies in European Urban History (1100–1800). Turnhout: Brepols, 63–82.

Haines, Margaret (1989). 'Brunelleschi and Bureaucracy: The Tradition of Public Patronage at the Florentine Cathedral', *I Tatti Studies in the Italian Renaissance*, 3: 89–125.

Hall, Marcia. (1979). *Renovation and Counter-Reformation: Vasari and Duke Cosimo in Santa Maria Novella and Santa Croce, 1565–1577*. Oxford University Press.

Harriss, Gerald L. (1975). *King, Parliament, and Public Finance in Medieval England to 1369*. Oxford University Press.

Hatcher, John. (1998). 'Labour, Leisure and Economic Thought before the Nineteenth Century', *Past & Present*, 160: 64–115.

Hatcher, John. (1986). 'Mortality in the Fifteenth Century', *Economic History Review*, 39: 19–38.

Hatcher, John. (2013). 'Unreal Wages: Long-Run Living Standards and the 'Golden Age' of the Fifteenth Century'. In Ben Dodds and Christian Liddy, eds. *Commercial Activity, Markets and Entrepreneurs in the Middle Ages: Essays in Honour of Richard Britnell*. Woodbridge: Boydell, 1–23.

Hatcher, John and Judy Stephenson, eds. (2019). *Seven Centuries of Unreal Wages: The Unreliable Data, Sources and Methods That Have Been Used for Measuring Standards of Living in the Past*. Cham: Springer.

Herlihy, David. (1997). *The Black Death and the Transformation of the West*, ed. Samuel Cohn Jr., Cambridge, MA.: Harvard University Press.

Herlihy, David. (1964). 'Direct and Indirect Taxation in Tuscan Urban Finance, ca. 1200–1400'. In *Finances et comptabilité urbaines du XIIIe au XVIe siècle*. Brussels: Pro Civitate, 1964, 385–405.

Herlihy, David. (1978). 'The Distribution of Wealth in a Renaissance Community: Florence 1427'. In P. Abrams and E.A. Wrigley, eds. *Towns in Societies: Essays in Economic History and Historical Sociology*. Cambridge University Press, 131–57.

Herlihy, David. (1967). *Medieval and Renaissance Pistoia: The Social History of an Italian Town*. New Haven: Yale University Press.

Herlihy, David. (1968). 'Santa Maria Impruneta: A Rural Commune in the Late Middle Ages'. In Nicolai Rubinstein, ed. *Florentine Studies. Politics and Society in Renaissance Florence*, Evanston: Northwestern University Press, 242–76.

Herlihy, David, and Christiane Klapisch-Zuber. (1978). *Les Toscans et leurs familles: Une étude du catasto florentin*. Paris: Presses de la foundation nationale des sciences politques.

Henderson, John. (2020). *Florence Under Siege: Surviving Plague in an Early Modern City*. New Haven: Yale University Press.

Henderson, John. (1988). 'The Parish and the Poor in Florence at the Time of the Black Death: The Case of S. Frediano', *Continuity and Change*, 3: 247–72.

Hills, Paul. (1990). 'The Renaissance Altarpiece: A Valid Category?' In P. Humfrey and M. Kemp, eds. *The Altarpiece in the Renaissance.* Cambridge University Press, 34–48.

Hilton, R.H. (1973). *Bond Men Made Free: Medieval Peasant Movements and the English Rising of 1381.* London: Temple Smith.

Hindle, Steve. (2000). *The State and Social Change in Early Modern England, 1550–1640.* Houndmills: Macmillan.

Holmes, Megan. (2011). 'Miraculous Images in Renaissance Florence', *Art History*, 34: 432–65.

Holmes, Megan. (2003). 'Neri di Bicci and the Commodification of Artistic Values in Florentine Painting (1450–1500)'. In M. Fantoni, L.C. Matthew, and S.F. Matthews-Grieco, eds. *The Art Market in Italy, 15th-17th Centuries,* Modena: Franco Cosimo Panini, 213–23.

Hughes, Diane. (1986). 'Representing the Family: Portraits and Purposes in Early Modern Italy', *Journal of Interdisciplinary History* 17: 929–52.

Humfrey, Peter and Richard MacKenney. (1986). 'The Venetian Trade Guilds as Patrons of Art in the Renaissance', *The Burlington Magazine*, 128: 317–30.

Imberciadori, Ildebrando. (1951). *Mezzadria classica Toscana: con documentazione inedita dal IX al XIV secolo.* Florence: Vallecchi.

Jacobs, Fredrika. (2013). *Votive Panels and Popular Piety in Early Modern Italy.* Cambridge University Press.

Jones, P.J. (1997). *The Italian City-State: From Commune to Signoria.* Oxford University Press.

Judde de Larivière, Claire and Rosa Salzberg. (2013). 'Le peuple est la cité: L'idée de popolo et la condition des popolani à Venise (XVe-XVIe siècles)', *Annales. Histoire, Sciences Sociales*, 68: 1113–40.

Judde de Larivière, Claire and Maartje Van Gelder, eds. (2020). *Popular Politics in an Aristocratic Republic: Political Conflict and Social Contestation in Late Medieval and Early Modern Venice.* London: Routledge.

Kent, D.V. (2000). *Cosimo de' Medici and the Florentine Renaissance: The Patron's Oeuvre.* New Haven: Yale University Press.

Kent, D.V. (1978). *The Rise of the Medici: Faction in Florence, 1426–1434.* Oxford University Press.

Kent, F.W. (1994). 'Lorenzo ... Amico degli uomin da bene: Lorenzo de' Medici and Oligarchy'. In Gian Carlo Garfagnini, ed. *Lorenzo il Magnifico e il suo mondo: Convegno internazionale di studi (Firenze 9–13 giugno 1992)*. Florence: Olschki, 43–60.

Kent, F.W. (2002). '"Be Rather Loved Than Feared": Class Relations in Quattrocento Florence'. In William Connell, ed., *Society and Individual in Renaissance Florence*. Berkeley: University of California Press, 13–50.

Kent, F.W. (1987a). 'Renaissance Patronage: An Introductory Essay'. In F. W. Kent and Patricia Simons, eds. *Patronage, Art, and Society in Renaissance Italy*. Oxford University Press, 1–21.

Kent, F.W. (1987b). 'Ties of Neighbourhood in Quattrocento Florence'. In F. W. Kent and Patricia Simons, eds. *Patronage, Art, and Society in Renaissance Italy*. Oxford University Press, 79–98.

Kent, F.W. (2005). 'Unheard Voices from the Medici Family Archive in the Time of Lorenzo de' Medici'. In F.W. Kent and Charles Zika, eds. *Rituals, Images, and Words: Varieties of Cultural Expression in Late Medieval and Early Modern Europe*. Late Medieval and Early Modern Studies, 3. Turnhout: Brepols, 389–404.

Killerby, Catherine Kovesi. (2002). *Sumptuary Law in Italy, 1200–1500*. Oxford University Press.

Klapisch-Zuber, Christiane. (1986). 'Women Servants in Florence during the Fourteenth and Fifteenth Centuries'. In Barbara Hanawalt, ed. *Women and Work in Preindustrial Europe*. Bloomington: Indiana University Press, 56–80.

Klassen, John. (1990). 'The Disadvantaged and the Hussite Revolution', *International Review of Social History*, 35: 249–72

Kuznets, Simon. (1955). 'Economic Growth and Income Inequality', *American Economic Review*, 45 (1): 1–28.

Labrouse, Camille-Ernest. (1944). *La crise de l'économie française à la fin de l'ancien régime et au début de la Revolution*. Paris: P.U.F.

la Roncière, Charles-M. (1976). *Florence, centre économique regional au XIVe siècle*, 5 vols. Aix-en-Provence: S.O.D.E.B.

la Roncière, Charles-M. (1982). *Prix et salaires à Florence au XIVe siècle (1280–1380)*. Rome: École française de Rome.

Le Roy Ladurie, Emmanuel. (1966). *Les paysans de Languedoc*, 2 vols. Paris: De Gruyter Mouton.

Leverotti, Franca. (1992). *Popolazione, famiglie, insediamento: Le sei miglia lucchesi nel XIV e XV secolo*. Ospedaletto (Pisa): Pacini.

Liddy, Christiane. (2005). *War, Politics and Finance in Late Medieval English Towns: Bristol, York and the Crown, 1350–1400*. Woodbridge: Boydell.

Lobel, M.D. (1935). *The Borough of Bury St. Edmund's: A Study in the Government and Development of a Monastic Town*. Oxford University Press.

Lopez, Robert. (1953). 'Hard Times and Investment in Culture'. In *The Renaissance: A Symposium, February 8–10,1952*. New York: The Metropolitan Museum of Art, 19–34.

Lopez, Robert and Harry A. Miskimin. (1962). 'The Economic Depression of the Renaissance', *Economic History Review*, 14: 408–26.

Mackenney, Richard. (1987). *Tradesmen and Traders: The World of the Guilds in Venice and Europe, c. 1250–c.1650*. London: Croom Helm.

Malanima, Paolo. (2013). 'When Did England Overtake Italy? Medieval and Early Modern Divergence in Prices and Wages', *European Review of Economic History*, 17: 45–70.

Mallett, Michael. (1989). 'Premessa: *Lettere* ai volumi V e VI'. In Michael Mallett, ed. *Lorenzo de' Medici Lettere V: 1480–81*. Florence: Giunti Gruppo.

Martines, Lauro. (2005). 'The Authority of Violence: Notes on Renaissance Florence'. In Elodie Lecuppre-Desjardin and Anne-Laure Van Bruaene, eds. *Emotions in the Heart of the City (14th–16th Century)*. Studies in European Urban History (1100–1800). Turnhout: Brepols, 31–40.

Meek, Cristine. (1978). *Lucca, 1369–1400: Politics and Society in an Early Renaissance City-State*. Oxford University Press.

Milanovic, Branko. (2019). 'Income Level and Income Inequality in the Euro-Mediterranean Region, c.14–700'. *Review of Income and Wealth*, 65 (1): 1–20.

Militzer, Klaus. (1980). *Ursachen und Folgen der innerstädtischen Auseinandersetzungen in Köln in der zweiten Hälfte des 14. Jahrhunderts*. Cologne: Wamper.

Moisé, Filippo. (1845). *Santa Croce di Firenze: Illustrazione storico-artistica*. Florence: [published at the author's expense].

Molà, Luca. (1994). *La comunità dei lucchesi a Venezia: immigrazione e industria della seta nel tardo Medioevo*, Memorie, Classe di Scienze morali, Lettere, ed Arte, 53. Venice: Istituto veneto di Scienze, Lettere ed Arti, 24–36.

Molho, Anthony. (1968a). 'The Florentine Oligarchy and the Balia of the Late Trecento', *Speculum*, 43: 23–51.

Molho, Anthony. (1968b). 'Politics and the Ruling Class in Early Renaissance Florence', *Nuova rivista storica*, 52: 401–20.

Muir, Edward. (1993). *Mad Blood Stirring: Vendetta and Factions in Friuli during the Renaissance*. Baltimore: Johns Hopkins University Press.

Munro, John. (1994). 'Urban Wage Structures in Late-medieval England and the Low Countries: Work-time and Seasonal Wages'. In I. Blanchard, ed. *Labour and Leisure in Historical Perspective*. Stuttgart: Franz Steiner, 65–78.

Munro, John. (2003). 'Wage-stickiness, Monetary Changes, and Real Incomes in Late-medieval England and the Low Countries, 1350–1500: Did Money Matter?' *Research in Economic History*, 21 (2003): 185–297.

Najemy, John. (2000). 'Civic Humanism and Florentine Politics'. In James Hankins, ed. *Renaissance Civic Humanism: Reappraisals and Reflections*. Cambridge University Press, 75–104.

Najemy, John. (1991). 'The Dialogue of Power in Florentine Politics'. In Anthony Molho and Kurt Raaflaub, eds. *City States in Classical Antiquity and Medieval Italy: Athens and Rome, Florence and Venice*. Ann Arbor: University of Michigan Press, 269–88.

Najemy, John. (2006a). 'Florentine Politics and Urban Spaces'. In Rodger Crum and John Paoletti, eds. *Renaissance Florence: A Social History*, Cambridge University Press, 19–54.

Najemy, John. (2006b). *A History of Florence 1200–1575*. Malden, MA: Blackwell Publishing.

Nelson, Jonathan and Richard Zeckhauser (2008). *The Patron's Payoff: Conspicuous Commissions in Italian Renaissance Art*. Princeton University Press.

North, Douglas C. and Robert Paul Thomas. (1973). *The Rise of the Western World: A New Economic History*. Cambridge University Press.

O'Malley, Michelle. (2005). *The Business of Art: Contracts and the Commissioning Process in Renaissance Italy*. New Haven: Yale University Press.

Orrman, Elias. (2003). 'The Condition of the Rural Population'. In Knut Helle, ed. *Cambridge History of Scandinavia*, 3 vols, I: *Prehistory to 1520*. Cambridge University Press, 581–610.

Padgett, John. (1993). 'Robust Action and the Rise of the Medici, 1400–1434', *American Journal of Sociology*, 98: 1259–317.

Pamuk, Şevket. (2007). 'The Black Death and the Origins of the 'Great Divergence' across Europe, 1300–1600', *European Review of Economic History*, 11: 289–317.

Parenti, Parenti. (1942). *Prezzi e mercato del grano a Siena (1546–1765)*. Florence: C. Cya.

Parenti, Giuseppe. (1939). *Prime richerche sulla rivoluzione dei prezzi a Firenze* Florence: C. Cya.

Park, Katherine. (1985). *Doctors and Medicine in Early Renaissance Florence*. Princeton University Press.

Petralia, Giuseppe. (2000). 'Fiscality, politics and dominion in Florentine Tuscany at the end of the Middle Ages'. In William Connell and Andrea Zorzi, eds. *Florentine Tuscany: Structures and Practices of Power*. Cambridge University Press, 65–89.

Plazzotta, Carol, Michele O'Malley, Ashok Roy, Raymond White, and Martin Wyld. (2006). 'The *Madonna di Loreto*: An Altarpiece by Perugino for Santa Maria dei Servi, Perugia', *National Gallery Technical Bulletin*, 27: 72–95.

Piketty, Thomas. (2020). *Capital and Ideology*, trans. Arthur Goldhammer. Cambridge, MA: Harvard University Press [French orig.: 2019].

Piketty, Thomas. (2014). *Capital in the Twenty-First Century*. Cambridge, MA: Harvard University Press [French orig. 2013].

Pinelli, P. (1999). *Prezzi e salari a Prato nel XIV secolo: Contributo alla determinazione delle condizioni di vita nel secolo della Peste Nera*. Pisa: Tesi Dottorale.

Pinto, Giuliano. (1981). 'I livelli di vita dei salariati cittadini nel periodo successivo al Tumulto dei Ciompi (1380–1430)'. In *Il Tumulto dei Ciompi: Un momento di storia Fiorentina ed Europea*. Florence: Olschki, 161–198.

Pinto, Giuliano. (1974). 'Il personale, le balie e i salariati dell'ospedale di San Gallo di Firenze negli anni 1395–1406: Note per la storia del salariato nelle città medievali', *Ricerche Storiche*, 4: 113–68.

Pinto, Giuliano and Paolo Pirillo, eds. (2013). *I Centri Minori della Toscana nel Medioevo: Atti del convegno internazionale di stui, Figline Valdarno, 23–23 ottobre 2009*. Biblioteca Storica Toscana a cura della Deputazione di Storia Patria per la Toscana, LXIX. Florence: Olschki.

Pope-Hennessy, John. (1966). *The Portrait in the Renaissance*. Bolligen Series, 35 Washington: National Gallery of Art.

Pope-Hennessey, John and Keith Christiansen. (1980). *Secular Painting in 15th-century Tuscany: Birth Trays, Cassone Panels, and Portraits*. New York: Metropolitan Museum of Art.

Postan, M.M. (1966). 'Medieval Agrarian Society in its Prime: England'. In M. M. Postan, ed. *Cambridge Economic History of Europe*, I, 2nd ed. Cambridge University Press, 549–632.

Postan, M.M. and John Hatcher. (1978). 'Population and Class Relations in Feudal Society', *Past & Present*, 8: 24–37.

Prescott, Andrew. (1984). Judicial Records of the Rising of 1381. PhD thesis, Bedford College, University of London.

Prestwich, Michael. (1980). *The Three Edwards: War and State in England 1272–1377*. London: Weidenfeld and Nicolson.

Putnam, Bertha (1908). *The Enforcement of the Statutes of Labourers during the First Decade after the Black Death 1349–1359*, Studies in History, Economics and Public Law, XXXII. New York: Columbia University.

Rainey, Ronald. (1985). Sumptuary Legislation in Renaissance Florence. PhD thesis, Columbia University.

Reis, Jaime. (2017). 'Deviant Behaviour? Inequality in Portugal 1565–1770', *Cliometrica* 11: 297–319.

Rexroth, Frank. (2007). *Deviance and Power in Late Medieval London*, trans. Pamela Selwyn. Cambridge University Press.

Rigby, Steven. (1998). 'Urban "Oligarchy" in Late Medieval England'. In J.A. F. Thomson, ed. *Towns and Townspeople in the Fifteenth Century*. Gloucester: Sutton, 62–86.

Robertson, Ian. (1985). 'Cesena: Governo e società dal Sacco dei Bretoni al dominio di Cesare Borgia'. In A. Vasina, ed. Storia di Cesena, II: Il medioevo, 2 (secoli XIV–XV). Rimini: Ghigi, 5–92.

Robertson, Ian (1987). 'Neighbourhood Government in Malatesta Cesena'. In F.W. Kent and Patricia Simons, eds. *Patronage, Art, and Society in Renaissance Italy*. Oxford University Press, 99–110.

Robertson, Ian. (2002). *Tyranny under the Mantle of St Peter: Pope Paul II and Bologna*, Late Medieval and Early Modern Studies, 5. Turnhout: Brepols.

Romano, Dennis. (2020). 'Popular Protest and Alternative Visions of the Venetian Polity, c. 1260–1423'. In Claire Judde de Larivière and Maartje Van Gelder, eds. *Popular Politics in an Aristocratic Republic: Political Conflict and Social Contestation in Late Medieval and Early Modern Venice*. London: Routledge, 22–44.

Rosenthal, David. (2006). 'The Spaces of Plebeian Ritual and the Boundaries of Transgression'. In Rodger Crum and John Paoletti, eds. *Renaissance Florence: A Social History*. Cambridge University Press, 161–81.

Sandri, Lucia. (1991). 'Ballatico mercenario e abbandono dei bambini alle istituzioi assistenziali: Un medesimo disagio sociale?' In Maria Giuseppina Muzzarelli, Paola Galetti, and Bruno Andreolli, eds. *Donne e lavoro nell'Italia medievale*. Turin: Rosenberg & Sellier, 93–104.

Scheidel, Walter (2017). *The Great Leveller: Violence and the Global History of Inequality from the Stone Age to the Present*. Oxford University Press.

Scheidel, Walter and Steven J. Friesen (2009). 'The Size of the Economy and the Distribution of Income in the Roman Empire', *The Journal of Roman Studies*, 99: 61–9.

Scott, Tom. (2012). *The City-State in Europe 1000–1600: Hinterland – Territory – Region*. Oxford University Press.

Seidel, Max. (1994). 'The Social Status of Patronage and its Impact on Pictorial Language in Fifteenth-Century Siena'. In E. Borsook and F. Superbi Gioffredi, eds. *Italian altarpieces, 1250–1550: Function and Design*. Oxford: Clarendon Press, 119–29.

Sherer, Idan. (2017). *Warriors for a Living: The Experience of the Spanish Infantry in the Italian Wars, 1494–1559*. Leiden: Brill.

Smith, Richard M. (2017). 'Contrasting Susceptibility to Famine in Early Fourteenth- and Late Sixteenth-century England: The Significance of Late Medieval Rural Social Structural and Village Governmental Changes'. In Michael J. Braddick and Phil Withington, eds. *Popular Culture and Political Agency in Early Modern England and Ireland*. Woodbridge: Boydell, 35–54.

Solórzano Telechea, Jesús. (2014). 'Protestas del común y cambio politico y cambio politico en las villas portuarias de la España atlántica a finales de la Edad Media'. In Hipólito Rafael Oliva Herrer, Vincent Challet, Jan Dumolyn, and María Antonia Carmona Ruiz, eds. *La Comunidad Medieval como esfera pública*. Seville: Secretaiado de publicaciones Vniversidad de Sevilla, 45–72.

Stuart, Susan Mosher. (2006). *Gilding the Market: Luxury and Fashion in Fourteenth-Century Italy*. Philadelphia: University of Pennsylvania Press.

Tognetti, Sergio. (2005). 'The Development of the Florentine Silk Industry: A Positive Response to the Crisis of the Fourteenth Century', *Journal of Medieval History*, 31: 55–69.

Tognetti, Sergio. (1995). 'Prezzi e salari nella Firenze tardomedievale: un profilo', *Archivio Storico Italiano*, 153: 263–333.

Trenholme, Norman Maclaren. (1927). *The English Monastic Boroughs: A Study in Medieval History*, entire issue of *University of Missouri Studies*, 3.

Trexler, R.C. (1972). 'Florentine Religious Experience: The Sacred Image', *Studies in the Renaissance*, 29: 7–41.

Trexler, R.C. (1980). *Public Life in Renaissance Florence*. Baltimore: Johns Hopkins University Press.

Tucker, Penelope. (2007). *Law Courts and Lawyers in the City of London, 1300–1550*. Cambridge University Press.

Van Os, Henk. (1987). 'Painting in a House of Glass: The Altarpieces of Pienza.' *Simiolus* 17(1): 23–38.

Van Zanden, Jan Luiten (1995). 'Tracing the Beginning of the Kuznets Curve: Western Europe during the Early Modern Period', *Economic History Review* 48(4): 643–64.

Vigo, Giovanni. (1974). 'Real Wages and the Working Class in Italy: Building Workers' Wages (14th to 18th century)', *Journal of European Economic History*, 3: 378–99.

Wackernagel, Martin (1981). *The World of the Florentine Renaissance Artist: Projects and Patrons, Workshop and Art Market*, transl. Alison Luchs. Princeton University Press [Leipzig, 1938].

Walter, John. (2006). *Crowds and Popular Politics in Early Modern England*. Manchester University Press.

Warburg, Aby. (1966). *La rinascita del paganesimo antico*. Florence: La nouva Italia [Gesammelte Schriften, 1932].

Weinbaum, Martin. (1937). *The Incorporation of Boroughs*. Manchester University Press.

Williams, Gwyn A (1963). *Medieval London: From Commune to Capital*. London: Athlone.

Williamson, Jeffrey G., and Peter H. Lindert (1980). *American Inequality: A Macro Economic History*. New York: Academic Press.

Wisch, Barbara and Diane Cole Ahl (eds.). (2000). *Confraternities and the Visual Arts in Renaissance Italy: Ritual, Spectacle, Image*. Cambridge University Press.

Wood, Andy. (2008). *The 1549 Rebellions and the Making of Early Modern England*. Cambridge University Press.

Wrightson, Keith. (1982). *English Society, 1580–1680*. London: Unwin Hyman.

Wunder, Heide. (1978). 'Peasant Organization and Class Conflict in East and West Germany', *Past & Present*, 78: 47–55.

Yerushalmi, Yosef Hayim. (1976). *The Lisbon Massacre of 1506 and the Royal Image in the 'Shebet Yehudah'*. Cincinnati: Hebrew Union College.

Zanetti, Dante. (1964). *Problemi alimentari di una economia preindustriale-ceriale a Pavia dal 1398 al 1700*. Turin: Boringhieri.

Acknowledgements

I thank the series editors, John Henderson and Jonathon Nelson, for their diligence and patience in reading my drafts, and the two external readers for their criticisms and willingness to approve a work that raises more questions than it solves. I thank two true authorities in inequality studies, past and present, for reading this Element: the sociologist Martin Sanchez-Jankowski at Berkeley, and the historical demographer Guido Alfani at the Bocconi. Finally, I thank Richard Bapty of the University of Glasgow Library for ordering online books for me during lockdown.

Cambridge Elements ≡

The Renaissance

John Henderson
Birkbeck, University of London, and Wolfson College, University of Cambridge

John Henderson is Professor of Italian Renaissance History at Birkbeck, University of London, and Emeritus Fellow of Wolfson College, University of Cambridge. His recent publications include *Florence Under Siege: Surviving Plague in an Early Modern City* (2019), *Plague and the City*, edited with Lukas Engelmann and Christos Lynteris (2019), and *Representing Infirmity: Diseased Bodies in Renaissance Italy*, edited with Fredrika Jacobs and Jonathan K. Nelson (2021). He is also the author of *Piety and Charity in Late Medieval Florence* (1994); *The Great Pox: The French Disease in Renaissance Europe*, with Jon Arrizabalaga and Roger French (1997); and *The Renaissance Hospital: Healing the Body and Healing the Soul* (2006).

Jonathan K. Nelson
Syracuse University Florence, and Kennedy School, Harvard University

Jonathan K. Nelson teaches Italian Renaissance Art at Syracuse University, Florence, and is research associate at the Harvard Kennedy School. His books include *Filippino Lippi* (2004, with Patrizia Zambrano), *Leonardo e la reinvenzione della figura femminile* (2007), *The Patron's Payoff: Conspicuous Commissions in Italian Renaissance Art* (2008, with Richard J. Zeckhauser); and he co-edited *Representing Infirmity. Diseased Bodies in Renaissance Italy* (2021). He co-curated museum exhibitions dedicated to Michelangelo (2002), Botticelli and Filippino (2004), Robert Mapplethorpe (2009), and Marcello Guasti (2019), and two online exhibitions about Bernard Berenson (2012, 2015). Forthcoming publications include a monograph on Filippino (Reaktion Books, 2022) and an Element, *The Risky Business of Renaissance Art.*

Assistant Editor

Sarah McBryde, *Birkbeck, University of London*

Editorial Board

Jane Tylus, *Yale University*
Kate van Orden, *Harvard University*

About the Series
Timely, concise, and authoritative, Elements in the Renaissance showcases cutting-edge scholarship by both new and established academics. Designed to introduce students, researchers, and general readers to key questions in current research, the volumes take multi-disciplinary and transnational approaches to explore the conceptual, material, and cultural frameworks that structured Renaissance experience.

Cambridge Elements ⌶

The Renaissance

Printed in the United States
by Baker & Taylor Publisher Services